The Secret Formula

JOSEPH MURPHY'S GOLDEN LESSONS

The Secret Formula

Discover Your Greater Self—
And Revolutionize Your Life

by Joseph Murphy

Author of *The Power of Your Subconscious Mind*

Edited by
Mitch Horowitz

MEDIA

Published 2021 by Gildan Media LLC
aka G&D Media
www.GandDmedia.com

Front cover design by David Rheinhardt of Pyrographx

Interior design by Meghan Day Healey of Story Horse, LLC

Library of Congress Cataloging-in-Publication Data is available
upon request

ISBN 978-1-7225-0553-0

10   9   8   7   6   5   4   3   2   1

CONTENTS

PREFACE:
"MAN'S GREATEST NEED"

"Man's greatest need is to believe in himself."

With this statement, Joseph Murphy opens this collection. I believe in his statement with all my heart. Faith in self is *not* our only need. But it is our most primal, basic, and promising. Without healthful self-belief—which is, by its nature, constructive and active rather than myopic and delusive—literally no enterprise would be possible.

This collection is about cultivation of purposeful self-confidence. A confidence born not necessarily from current ability so much as potential ability. A confidence arising from the realization that your mind itself is the mediator of greater laws and forces, which make you a creative being. A confidence that is not hubristic but that is composed, persistent, and certain that mental effort will eventually open all roads. A confidence that fosters authentic self-measure and not fanciful arrogance. A confidence that is truth.

The formula for this kind of confidence does not come cheaply. It requires, Murphy writes, intention, dedication, persistence, and focus. Your mind will not yield its fruits to you without those efforts. But with them, you will, as a seeker, discover that you have every reason to feel confident. Because you will discover the existence of a greater, nonlocal mind of which your private intellect is a channel and a means of creative co-expression.

.   .   .

We often think of the subconscious as a hidden engine of events, both good and bad. And that's valid enough. But in this collection—and this is part of the "secret formula" in its title—Murphy urges you to also understand your subconscious *as a friend and ally*. By using the methods Murphy provides, including acts of self-suggestion just before drifting to sleep each night, you will learn how to program your subconscious to assist you with ideas, workable plans, and fresh insights. Your subconscious is, in large measure, your destiny. And your destiny can be shaped.

.   .   .

Murphy also observes in this collection that the world believes in "lies." These lies are the conditioned limits that get engendered in us in childhood and reinforced by conformist peer opinion and underdeveloped self-image. These socially approved lies cement in us an emotional conviction that hurtful experiences of the past must necessarily repeat, or that some kind of negative cause-and-effect is stacked against us. Murphy urges you to take a sledgehammer to that outlook. He cites numerous examples—including from the lives of compelling and contemporaneous peers such as psychologist Viktor Frankl—that many limitations are, in large measure, self-created and not part of the natural order of life.

"Change this moment," Murphy writes, "and you change your destiny." That is the simple, compelling truth of this book. And the best way to alter the present moment is to alter your conception of self. You have every reason to upend and strengthen your sense of self. This book is a beacon toward experiment and new experience in that direction. May it bring you a greater estimate of who you really are.

—*Mitch Horowitz*

Adjust to Wealth
and Health

Man's greatest need is to believe in himself, in what he is doing, and in his ultimate destiny. Self-reliance or self-confidence finds its greatest outlet when it is accompanied by a belief that the real self of man is God and that with God, all things are possible.

Shakespeare wrote about the divinity which shapes your ends, rough-hew it how you will. The Bible gives the key to building spiritual self-reliance, but without faith, it is impossible to please him, for he that cometh to God must first believe that God is and that He is a rewarder of them that diligently seek Him.

Down through the ages, all men and women who have possessed spiritual self-reliance have had a deep, abiding conviction that they were one with the God presence within. God is the living spirit within you. God is spirit, and they that worship Him worship Him in spirit and in truth. His spirit has no face, form, or figure. It's timeless, shapeless, and ageless.

You worship no man. You give your attention, your devotion, your loyalty to the spirit within you which created the universe and created you. It's all-powerful, knows all, and sees all. When you're in tune with Him, that infinite power responds to you, and you do marvelous things.

Great men down through the ages were sure of themselves without being aggressive, egotistical, or intolerant. Jesus, Moses, Buddha, Lao-tzu, Confucius, Mohammad, many others accomplished the so-called impossible through the absolute conviction that they could do what they set out to do through the divine power which strengthened and inspired them. They were all men born like you were.

You can accomplish little in this world without faith. The farmer when he plants his seed has faith in the science of agriculture. The chemist has faith in the laws and principles of chemistry. The doctor has faith in his knowledge of anatomy, physiology, *materia medica*, and pharmacology. He has faith in his skill as a surgeon. The engineer has implicit faith in the laws of mathematics, stress and strain, and other principles of the universe. Then he builds a building according to scientific laws which existed before any man walked the earth or before any church was ever formed.

You can have the same abiding faith in the laws of your own mind, which are the same yesterday, today, and forever. A man who thinks that the principles of chemistry and physics and mathematics are different than the principles and laws operating in his own mind is living in the Dark Ages. These mental and spiritual laws are just as dependable and undeviating as the laws of gravitation, Boyle's law, or Avogadro's law.

We know for a fact that if you think good, then good follows; and if you think evil, then evil follows. If you think of yourself as a failure, and you picture a failure, you will fail. Think of success and realize you're born to succeed and to win, for the infinite cannot fail. Picture yourself successful, happy, and free, and you will be.

Whatever you think and feel is true, and your conscious mind is embodied in your subconscious and comes to pass into your experience. That's the law of mind: undeviating, immutable, timeless, and changeless. We're not talking about faith in creeds or dogmas or traditions or any religious persuasion. We're talking about faith in your own thoughts, in your own feelings, in the laws of your own mind, and the goodness of God in the land of the living. Faith in that creative intelligence which responds to your thought.

You can have faith that you're going to be ill when exposed to a draft, or that you will catch a virus or a severe cold because someone sneezes in your presence. You can have faith that you will fail, and your business ventures will turn out badly. But your faith is in the wrong thing, isn't it?

A woman once said to me, "For ten years I had absolute faith I would be alone through life. No one would marry me, and I would be poor and miserable. Then I read a book, *The Power of your Subconscious Mind*," a book I wrote many years ago, "and I applied the prayers outlined. Now, I am happily married, have a marvelous husband, and have been blessed with three lovely children." This woman reversed her faith in the negative to a joyous expectancy of the best in all phases of her life.

Fear is faith in the wrong thing. Fear is faith upside down. Have faith in the goodness of God in the land of the living. Have faith in divine love. Have faith in the healing presence which made you to heal you. The law of this woman's mind responded to her belief, for the law of life is the law of belief.

What do you believe in? To believe is to accept something as true. Believe in whatsoever things are true, whatsoever things are lovely, whatsoever things are just, whatsoever things are pure, whatsoever things are of good rapport. If there be any virtue, if there be any praise, believe in these things.

The first step in building self-reliance or self-confidence is to believe in that infinite power within you which grows hair on your face, digests your food, grows your nails when you're sound asleep, and grows hair on your head. It watches over you when you are sound asleep. It governs your heartbeat and all the vital organs of your body, and all the processes of your body are controlled by that infinite intelligence. That's what we're talking about.

For example, if you cut yourself, it heals you. If you burn yourself, it reduces the edema, gives you new tissue and skin. It always seeks to heal you. That's the life principle in you, and you know you're alive, you know you have a mind, and you know you have that spirit because you can feel the spirit of joy and rapture and ecstasy and love when you look into your child's eye. All these are invisible, yet they're real.

So, believe in that infinite power within you. Recognize and know that the self of you is God. That's your higher self, the living spirit within you that was never born, will never die. Water wets it not, fire burns it not, wind blows it not away. It's eternal. It is the very life principle in you, through you, and all around you.

The second step is to commune regularly with this infinite presence and power, and have a vision realizing you go where your vision is. Your vision is what you're mentally looking at, what you're giving attention to, what you're thinking quietly, silently, and feelingly at this moment. That's where you're going, and that's what's going to happen to you.

Let your vision be of abundance, right action, inspiration, and divine guidance, and you will become like the perennial mountain of snow, which when melted by the heat of the sun blows downward like a river of life giving nourishment and sustenance to the valleys.

What difference does it make if you have foundered and failed many times, now that you know the divine presence indwells you, and the infinite intelligence and infinite power and the infinite life principle is the God presence within you? You know that it responds to you. One should be happy.

Stand up that divine gift within you. Wake up the sleeping giant within you. Trust that creative intelligence within you, more so than you ever trusted your human father or mother. When the thought comes to you, *I cannot do this,* affirm that the divine presence can. It's the infinite presence. It's the infinite power. There's nothing to oppose it or challenge it. It is Almighty.

If the thought comes, look at all the difficulties and obstructions. Realize and know and say "bully" to yourself. Infinite intelligence and infinite power know no obstructions, delays, or impediments. Find an affirmation which counteracts all your negations, and your life will become more blessed and beautiful through the years.

You will find your obstructions and challenges will be transformed into opportunities. Your fear will turn to faith, and your doubt will turn into certainty that the infinite healing presence is within you, and wonders happen as you tune in upon it.

• • •

I had an intensely interesting conversation with a hotel proprietor in Lisbon, Portugal. He told me that he had started out as a waiter in a small restaurant, and when the boss would ask him to do something special, he would say, "I am going to try to do it."

His boss finally said to him, "Never say 'I'm going to try.' Say, 'I am going to do it,' and know that you can do it. Then, the power will respond to you."

He said, "I profited from that advice, and I never again said 'I'm going to try.' I began to believe in myself. I know that infinite power indwells me, for the Bible says the kingdom of God or intelligence is within you." His secret was *"I'm going to do it."*

He began to affirm, perhaps a thousand times a day, "I'm going to have a big hotel, and own it." He believed that through the power of the infinite he would do exactly that.

"The answer came in a strange way," he continued. "I won at roulette in Monaco, the equivalent of $100,000 in American money. I opened this hotel, and now I have paid off the mortgage. I have prospered beyond my fondest dreams."

This man said he had felt an overwhelming urge to go to the tables in Monaco, and he asked a friend to accompany him and show him the ropes. He knew he would win. It was an inner, silent knowing of the soul. He had fabulous winnings, and when he had enough money, $100,000 for a deposit on his hotel, he stopped and never gambled again. This was the way his subconscious mind answered his prayer for a hotel of his own.

The ways of your subconscious are neutral. Money is just an idea, a symbol of exchange. There is nothing evil in the universe and nothing good or bad, but thinking makes it so. Good and evil are the movements of man's own mind relative to the infinite life principle within him, which is forever perfect, whole, and complete in itself.

Make up your mind now this minute that you can do what you want to do and can be what you sincerely want to be and can have what you wish to possess. It will be done to you as you believe. Follow the age-old maxim, "Be sure you are right. Then, go ahead." Let nothing move you or shake your conviction. Make it a part of your mentality. With this kind of belief, you will inevitably succeed and move forward in life.

What is it that the immensely wealthy man or the prominent businessman possesses that you do not? Only one thing. It is self-reliance or self-confidence.

He believes in himself and the powers within him, both of which mean the same thing of course. Self-reliance or self-confidence are one. Confidence means "with faith," faith in a principle, in the powers of your mind. Just like an engineer has faith in the principles of mathematics, faith in the principle of strain and stress.

You meet men and women who have reached the top of their professions. They're successful in the art of living. They have marvelous homes. They have wonderful children. They're contributing to humanity in countless ways. They're successful in their prayer life, relationship with the divine, and relationships with people.

All this is due to their implicit trust in faith, in that inner power within them. They place their whole reliance on that infinite guiding principle, on the divine love, and the divine protection in all ways. Their words, actions, demeanor, and general attitude radiate power and confidence, and thus win your respect the first time you meet them.

Last year, I interviewed a man in Hilo, Hawaii. He was very wealthy, but he sadly said to me, "I am nobody. No one cares for me." Frankly, no one did, for the simple reason that he did not respect or care for the self within him. He was down on himself, and if you are cruel or mean to yourself, others will be cruel and mean to you, for as within, so without.

This man was down on himself even though he had vast holdings of real estate and large bank deposits. I explained to him that he was constantly criticizing and belittling himself, and that doing that, others must treat him the same way. If he expected to accomplish precisely nothing of himself, neither would anyone expect any more of him. For as within, so without. The inside controls the outside.

I pointed out to him that the riches of the infinite were within him and all around him. Shakespeare wrote, "All things be ready if the mind be so." All he had to do was to call on the infinite presence and power, and it would respond to his thought. He began to use some of the great eternal truths of the Bible, which I outlined for him as follows:

"Know ye not that ye are the temple of the living God and that the spirit of God dwelleth in you."

"But, the fruit of the spirit is love, joy, peace, patience, gentleness, goodness, faith, meekness, and temperance."

"Thou will keep Him in perfect peace whose mind is stayed on thee because he trusteth in thee."

"In all thy ways acknowledge Him, and He shall make plain thy paths."

"Trust Him, believe in Him, and He shall bring it to pass."

This is the way the Lord created you. Rejoice and be glad that infinite being created you, and know it is always with you, and is capable of healing you, restoring you, vitalizing and energizing you.

We know that all things work together for good to them that love God, to them who are called according to His purpose. God in the midst of you is healing you now.

Building
Self-Confidence

"Whatsoever a man soweth, that shall he also reap." Action and reaction are equal to each other. Ella Wheeler Wilcox expressed this law of mind as follows:

> "Give to the world the best you have, and the best will come back to you. Give love, and love to your heart will flow as strength in your utmost need. Have faith, and a score of hearts will show their faith in your word indeed, for life is a mirror of the king and the beggar. It is just what you are and do. Then, give to the world the best you have, and the best will come back to you."

To adjust is to fit, adapt, accommodate, regulate, to put in working order. In order to adjust to life, it is necessary that you become a channel through which the life principle flows freely, harmoniously, joyously, and lovingly. The solution to all your problems is to get acquainted with and use the divine presence and power in your life. Acquaint now thyself with Him and be at peace, and good shall come unto thee.

I suggest that each person establish a definite method of working and that he practice it regularly and systematically every day. For example, determine for yourself what is the most troublesome problem you have. Decide to solve this problem now by realizing that infinite intelligence within you knows the way out. Its nature is to respond to you. It knows only the answer, and the nature of infinite intelligence is responsiveness. That is your answer, as certain as the rising of the moon tonight.

●　　●　　●

A young man I met had experienced a poverty complex for many years and had received no answers to his prayers. He had prayed for prosperity, but the fear of poverty continuously weighed on his mind. Naturally, he attracted more lack and limitation. Your subconscious mind accepts the dominant of two ideas. This is a law. After talking with him, he learned to pray as follows:

"I know there is only one source, the life principle from which all things flow. It created the universe and all things are in contained. I am a focal point of the divine presence. My mind is open and receptive. I am a free-flowing channel for harmony, beauty, guidance, wealth, and the riches of the infinite. I know that wealth, health, prosperity, and success are released from within and appear on the without.

"I am now in harmony with the infinite supply, and just as I would adjust an instrument in my laboratory, I am now mentally adjusting my focused attention on the eternal source of all blessings. I wish for everyone all the blessings of life. I am open and receptive to God's riches, spiritual, mental, and material, and they flow to me in avalanches of abundance."

This young man changed his attitude of mind and focused on divine riches rather than poverty, and made it a special point not to deny what he affirmed. In a month's time his whole life was transformed. He affirmed the above truths morning and evening for about ten minutes, knowing that he was actually writing down these truths in his subconscious mind, causing the latter to be activated and to release the hidden treasures.

Whatever you impress on your subconscious mind is expressed on the screen of space, and your conscious mind is the pen, the thinker, and what you think and feel comes to pass.

Aristotle said, "Resistance is the cause of every monstrosity," and monstrosity in the body could be a growth, a tumor, a lesion, or any other abnormal condition.

I knew a woman who was resenting and hating her ex-husband. In addition, her physician told her she had developed a serious lesion. She was resisting the free flow of the life principle which flows as harmony, beauty, joy, and love. In other words, the life more abundant. She was blocking the infinite, healing presence. She finally realized what she was doing and came to a clear-cut decision to pray as follows:

"I surrender my ex-husband to the God presence completely. Whenever he comes to my mind I affirm, 'God's love fills your mind and heart.'"

Then she adjusted her mind to the infinite healing presence, frequently claiming:

"The infinite healing presence which created me from a cell knows all the processes and functions of my body. It knows how to heal, for I am the Lord that healeth thee, and this healing love fills my mind and heart, and I am made whole and perfect."

At the end of three weeks, she returned for another examination by her doctor, and the lesion had disappeared. Divine love dissolves everything unlike itself.

•   •   •

There are people who resist the weather, new ideas, newspaper headlines, and even their neighbors. There always seems to be friction in their mental and physical relationships. *Happy is he who trusted in thee.* Adjustment takes place in your own mind when your thoughts are harmonious, peaceful, loving, and based on eternal verities.

In other words, when you get along with yourself, you will be able to get along with others. If your habitual thinking is based on resentment, fear, ill will, hostility, and/or self-condemnation, you will project your hostility and animosity onto others, and you will experience very poor relationships in your business, home, or professional work.

Learn to be pliable, flexible, and adjustable. If there is someone in your office who is obstreperous, petulant, and fractious, realize you did not create him. Lose him, and let him go mentally. You're not responsible for his warped or twisted mentality, and you should realize he has no power to disturb you. It's always a movement of your own thought which disturbs or annoys you.

Two thousand years ago, Marcus Aurelius said, "If the cucumber is bitter, don't eat it." Very simple, isn't it? Ask yourself, "What is my aim in life?" Let the answer be peace, harmony, and divine wisdom, because this is so. Identify with your aim and not with the boorishness or surliness of others. Repeat the following affirmation daily: "Divine peace and harmony, govern me and reign supreme in my life."

When you mentally and emotionally identify with your spiritual aim in life, nothing in the external world disturbs you. Stop giving power, prerogatives, and privileges to people who have no power. No one disturbs you but yourself. It's a movement of your own thought, your own emotions, your actions, and reactions. They all take place in your own mind.

Have you ever noticed the way water flows according to the line of least resistance? You may have watched a stream flowing down from a mountain. It never quarrels, fights, or resists the rocks, boulders, or obstacles in its way. The water goes around the boulders or flows over them and eventually finds its way back to the ocean. All the stumps, stones, and trees disappear or wear away since nothing can seriously impede the flow of the streams back to the ocean.

You are a river of life, and your purpose is to meet challenges, difficulties, and problems, and to overcome them. Not by mentally fighting or quarreling with them, but by meeting them head on while realizing that joy is in overcoming.

Say to yourself, *"The problem is here, but infinite intelligence within me is here also. It knows only the answer. This problem is divinely outmatched. I will grapple with this problem courageously and through the wisdom and the power of the infinite, I will overcome."* With that attitude, you will become victorious, and you will move onward and upward.

An engineer I know has a wonderful technique for meeting what he calls so-called insuperable obstacles. His constant prayer is, *"The streams of life, power, wisdom, intelligence, joy, and peace flow through me like a golden river revealing to me everything I need to know and giving me the strength to complete all assignments in divine order."*

He has made his adjustment with the life principle, and he has completed every assignment in divine order. Do not try to manipulate or change other people. Permit them to have their political or religious beliefs, their peculiarities, eccentricities, and abnormalities. Judge not, and where you have no judgment, you experience no suffering. Where there is no opinion, there is no suffering. Where there's no judgment, there is no pain.

Establish the right relationship to the life principle by realizing the life principle is always seeking to express itself through you as the life more abundant. If you are angry, hateful, resentful, or are engaging in self-condemnation or self-criticism, your foot is on the hose, and the waters of life do not flow through you. These negative emotions get snarled up in your subconscious mind and have negative outlets such as mental and physical disorders.

Become an open channel for the divine presence. Realize you're a focal point of the divine life, and like an electric bulb, you are here to let your light shine before men that they see your good works, thereby glorifying and revealing your faith in the infinite intelligence, and the infinite power and infinite life principle within you.

*   *   *

A lonely person has shut out friends from his life. He is not in tune with the infinite, and is usually nursing some psychic trauma, saying to himself, "I have been hurt before. I will not get friendly with people lest I get hurt again."

All this is foolishness. Every person is an epitome of the divine, and when you exalt the divinity in the midst of you and salute the divinity in others, you will automatically radiate friendship, love, and goodwill to all people, and you will never lack for friends. You must be a friend to have a friend.

How would something like this play out in the workplace? Do you think your coworkers should change and make the adjustment? There is no one to change but yourself. When you change, your world magically melts in the image and likeness of your contemplation.

If you are married, you and your spouse should adjust to each other's peculiarities and idiosyncrasies. Overlooking each other's shortcomings, but focusing on, and exalting, the qualities which endear you to each other. If you are in tune with the infinite and full of goodwill to all, there will be no friction or excess tension, and you will have no bodily disturbances.

A young woman was resisting life, complaining, "I am leading a humdrum existence. I am lonely, frustrated, and I have no friends. I lead a drab, weary existence." She learned that her thought is created and that by thinking along these lines, she was compounding her misery because whatever we give attention to, the subconscious magnifies.

After learning something of the laws of life, she reversed her mental attitude and began to affirm, frequently and habitually, *"I am happy, joyous, and free. I am loving, kind, harmonious, and peaceful. I sing the song of praise and joy in the Lord, which is my strength, for the Lord is that Lordly power within me, my mind, my spirit, which created me, the invisible part of me."*

She realized that whatever she attaches to "I am," she becomes, which is an age-old Hindu truth. Whatever you attach to I am, you become. You can say, "I'm poor, I'm deaf, I'm no good, I'm a flop, I'm a failure." You'll become all these things.

On the other hand, you can say, "I'm illumined, I'm inspired, I'm successful, I'm happy, joyous, and free." Feel it, believe it. She made a habit of affirming the above wonderful truths. Her whole life was changed from her former, so-called drab existence to fullness of life including marriage to a young dentist, a new home, and a new perspective and a new insight into the wonders of that infinite life principle within her.

         *   *   *

Let us have a meditation now. Know that the light dispels darkness. So does the love of the good overcome all evil. Love and hate cannot dwell together. Love casts out fear.

Turn the light of the infinite upon all fear or anxious thoughts in your mind, and they flee away. The dawn, the light of truth appears, and the shadows, fear, and doubt flee away. Know divine love watches over you, guides you, makes clear the path for you. Realize you're expanding into the divine. Divine love surrounds you, enfolds you, and enwraps you. Divine love grows before you today and every day, making joyous and glorious your way.

There is a miraculous healing power within you, that made you. This infinite healing presence is flowing through you now, vitalizing, energizing, cleansing, purifying your whole being, so that your whole body dances to the rhythm of the eternal God.

There Is
One Thing You
Cannot Have

There is one thing you cannot have, and that is something for nothing. As a professor said recently, "There is no such thing as a free lunch."

Some time ago I was in a store, and they offered a package of blades free if you bought two tubes of shaving cream. Of course they can't give the blades free, they're included in the overall price. Or it's included in the overall cost of running business or in the customer's charge.

Nothing is free. You must give your attention, devotion, and loyalty to some subject. Then you will get a response. "*Come to the waters and drink. Yea, he that hath no money, let him come. Buy wine and milk without money, without price.*" The price is recognition, price is belief, conviction. There's always a price to be paid. Nothing is free.

People say salvation is free. No, it isn't. "*By grace are ye saved through faith,*" Paul said. Grace simply means that the love, the light, and the glory of the infinite responds to any man when he calls it. "*Call upon me; I will answer you. I will be with you in trouble. I will set you on high because you hath known my name."*

Grace means the response of a supreme intelligence to your conscious thinking and acting. It's available to all men. It's not only for certain people because of religious affiliation or creed or dogma.

The nature of infinite intelligence is responsiveness. It responds to all men. When you tried to learn to walk, or when you learned to swim or to dance, you repeated a thought pattern act again and again, and now you say it's second nature. Second nature is the response of your subconscious mind to your conscious thinking and acting.

Just like how you drive an automobile. You no longer touch the car with intensity or grip the wheel with intensity, not at all. You touch it lightly, and actually it's your subconscious mind driving the car. In other words it's effortless effort, effort without tension or stress. You paid the price in attention, devotion, and loyalty to a principle and stick-to-itiveness and determination.

Now you're able to drive the car or ride the bicycle or swim or play music blindfolded. You repeated a thought pattern again and again with your fingers, and now you play automatically. It's your subconscious playing.

So we pay the price for everything. Recognition, acceptance, and conviction. Give your attention, your devotion, your loyalty to any subject and it will yield its secrets back to you. And if you do not give your attention to a particular subject, whether chemistry or physics or mathematics, you will remain in darkness regarding that particular subject.

* * *

I remember Mrs. Menier, a wonderful teacher in New York City. She lived in the Lucerne Hotel, where I lived for a time in New York. I used to speak with her occasionally.

She had a childhood friend who would come, listen to her, take the books, and all that, and she would borrow the old clothes that Mrs. Menier gave her, an old fur coat, umbrella, and things of that nature. I said to her one time, "Why doesn't this woman listen to you, to your teaching? She doesn't have to borrow old clothes."

"Well," she said, "she's unwilling to pay the price. She's unwilling to give attention, she's unwilling to apply these truths. She prefers old clothes to wisdom." I think Mrs. Menier was right. The friend preferred old clothes and secondhand umbrellas and such to the application of the mental and spiritual laws.

All she had to do was give attention, devotion, and interest to the great truths. But she was unwilling to pay the price, and that's true of many people. Ms. Menier was very sympathetic, and more or less kept on giving her these old clothes, which didn't do the friend any good.

At a summer seminar on "The Power of Your Subconscious Mind" in Denver some years ago, a woman said to me, "I could have anything I want if I only believed I had it in my mind."

She'd been praying for the healing of a skin condition for ten years with no results. She had applied various astringent lotions and other topical medication without any appreciable relief. I explained to her that the only thing one cannot have in life is something for nothing. You have to pay the price, and so she would have to pay that price. The price for healing is faith in the infinite healing presence, *"For according to your faith or belief is it done unto you."* The woman had never paid the price.

Faith is not in a creed or dogma or church or man or anything of that nature. If you have faith in chemistry, for example, don't you study the laws of chemistry, of attraction, repulsion, the law of valence, and so on? Of course you do, and you bring forth marvelous compounds which bless humanity in countless ways. Your faith grows as you give attention to the great principles of chemistry, which are the same yesterday, today, and forever.

Faith is attention, devotion, and loyalty to the one creative power. You have faith when you know thoughts are things. What you feel, you attract; what you imagine, you become. You have faith when you know that any idea emotionalized or felt as true is deposited in the subconscious mind and comes forth as form, function, experience, and event. Then you would have faith in the creative laws of your own mind. You would have faith that an infinite intelligence is responsive to your thought. When you call upon it, it answers you, and you have definite faith and belief in that.

For example, men have been lost in the jungle, and they had faith that they would be directed and guided out of the place. They had no compass or sextant, but some men sat down and said, *"The Lord is my shepherd, I shall not want. He leadeth me back to my battalion. He leads me to safety. He is guiding me now."* They followed the lead, that feeling that comes to men when you call on the supreme intelligence, and they were led oftentimes to the river. They would follow the riverbank, and then become rescued.

That's the guiding principle. They paid the price, didn't they? Recognition, attention to it, calling upon it because if you do not call upon it and recognize it, it's the same as if it were not there. For this infinite intelligence will do nothing for you except through you.

The price this woman had to pay was recognition of the power of the infinite, acceptance of that healing presence, and conviction that the healing is taking place now, *"For I am the Lord that healeth thee."* She had been giving power to externals, saying, "My skin is sensitive to the sun. I'm allergic to the cold weather. I believe this eczema is all over my arms due to heredity. My mother had a similar condition. It's my genes and chromosomes that are at fault."

Her mind was divided. She had never paid the price, which was to give her attention to the infinite healing presence and the law of her own subconscious, to trust that law and believe in the healing presence and that it would respond and come to pass. She began to pray as follows:

"The infinite healing presence which created my body and all its organs knows all the processes and functions of my body. I claim, feel, and know definitely and absolutely that the grandeur and glory of the infinite are made manifest in my mind and body. The wholeness, vitality, and life of the infinite flow through me now, and every atom of my being is transformed by the infinite healing presence.

"I fully and freely forgive everyone, and I pour out life, love, truth, and beauty to all my relatives and in-laws. I know that I have forgiven everyone because I can meet the person in my mind, and there is no longer any sting. I give thanks for the healing which is taking place now, and I know that when I call, the answer comes."

She repeated this prayer slowly, quietly, and reverently several times a day. She told me prior to my leaving Denver that a remarkable change for the better had come over her entire being, mentally and physically, and a complete healing began to take place before her eyes. She had to pay the price by steadying and readying her mind to receive the gift of healing. Heretofore her mind was divided in its allegiance as she was giving power to diets, the climate, heredity, and other factors.

The Bible says, *"Are you going to say it is hard for me? Is the Lord's hand shortened that he cannot save?"* She began to understand that the scientific thinker does not make the phenomenal world or any external thing a cause. The cause of all is the spirit within, the God presence. God is the first cause and all powerful, supreme, and omnipotent. Nothing to oppose it, challenge it, thwart it, or vitiate it.

The moment you postulate another power, you are divided in your mind, and your subconscious does not respond to your divided and confused mind. If you begin to press the up and down buttons in an elevator, you would not go up or down but remain where you are.

Faith comes through understanding the laws of your mind and applying them diligently in all your affairs. You can grow in faith in the same way that I mentioned previously, that a chemist grows in his knowledge of chemistry, the research bringing forth wonderful compounds for the alleviation of human misery as well as removing the drudgery of life.

Scientists are gradually growing in faith by constant research into nature and her laws, and they're accomplishing great things. The farmer has to deposit seeds in the ground in order to get a harvest. He must determine whether he's going to have wheat, oats, or barley. He makes a decision. He plants the seed in the ground. He has to give to get. He has to give to the soil. In order for you to receive, you must first give to your mind. Before you can receive wealth, you must first impress your subconscious mind with the idea of wealth, and whatever is impressed in the subconscious is expressed on the screen of space.

You have things by right of consciousness only. You must build the mental equivalent into your mentality of whatever it is you want. You do this by giving your attention and devotion to health or wealth, or peace or harmony, or anything that you want in life, for the infinite is within you. The gift has been given. God is the giver and the gift, and you're the receiver.

What can you give God? You can't give God anything. God is that infinite presence and power in all, over all, through all, the life principle, the progenitor, the Father of all. What on earth could you give the infinite? It's all things to all men. It's everything. It's the blade of grass. It's the apple. It's the air. It's the sea. It's everything.

The whole world was here when you were born. The only thing you can give God, or the living spirit in you, is recognition, honor, loyalty, and devotion. That's the only thing. "*Call upon me, I will answer you. I'll be with you in trouble. I'll set you on high because you hath known my name.*" The name is the nature of it. The nature is to respond to you.

You're told, "*Before you call, I will answer. While you're yet speaking, I will hear.*" The answer is already within you, to any problem under the sun. Intuition is within you. You can be taught from within. Telepathy is within you, clairvoyance, all these faculties are within you.

You can change your mind, your body, you can change everything. Change your thoughts and keep them changed. All that any person can desire is already present in the divine presence within you, in which you live and move and have your being. For God lives,

moves, and has being in you. God is the light principle, the progenitor, the living spirit Almighty within
you, for God is spirit. *"They that worship Him, worship
Him in spirit and in truth."*

The very fact that you desire something is proof
of the existence of that which you desire. The active
desiring on your part brings about a response from the
supreme intelligence within you. *"Your Father knoweth
what things you have need of before you ask."* The need is
already satisfied. The gift has been given, for God is
the giver and the gift, and you're the receiver.

"Son, thou art ever with me, and all that I have is thine."
"All things be ready if the mind be so."

Health is now, peace is now. The healing presence
is within you. Love is now, joy is now. Power is now.
Are you going to wait for the power of the Almighty
to flow through you? It's within you now. Say, "The
power of the Almighty is flowing through me now."
Are you going to wait for peace and say someday you'll
have peace of mind?

The God of peace is within you, and that river of
peace is flowing through you now. The gift is already
there. God is the giver and the gift. God indwells you.
"All things be ready if the mind be so." Accept peace and
poise now. Accept inspiration now, accept guidance
now. You must open your eyes, you must open your
heart, and receive. If you have something in both

hands, you must drop something to pick something else up.

You must get rid of the false beliefs in your mind and accept the truth, which is, "For all things are ready if the mind be so." You ready your mind to accept the gift, for *"I am the Lord that healeth thee."* The healing power of God is within you. It heals a cut on your finger. It's right there. The surgeon removes a tumor. He says, "Nature will heal you." He removes the block so you'll always get a response.

Perhaps you have experienced this as you try to solve a particular problem. You racked your brain, you asked others to help you. You read all the books. You tried to find a solution which the scientist or the chemist or the pharmacist sometimes does, or the doctor or the surgeon or the astrophysicist.

You struggle with the problem, you try to get an answer, and then you're exhausted. You give up, in a way, and turn it over to the deeper mind, and you go off to sleep, perhaps. Oftentimes the answer comes to you in a dream, in a vision of the night, or as you awaken in the morning. It pops into your mind like toast out of a toaster. This happens over and over and over again.

You pay the price: attention, devotion, loyalty, recognition of a supreme intelligence which knows only the answer. When you surrender, when you give up, when you turn it over, and say there is that within me that knows, then the answer comes.

You engaged a supreme intelligence, an infinite presence and power, and it responded to you. You gave it attention, and you got the answer.

●　●　●

Einstein loved mathematics and it revealed its secrets to him. He was engrossed and fascinated with the universe and its laws. The unified field theory came to him in a flash, like a flash of lightning into his conscious, reasoning mind. He gave his attention, devotion, and industry to the subject of time, space, and the fourth dimension. His subconscious responded by revealing the secrets of these subjects to him.

Edison experimented, meditated on, and explained the principle of electricity. He had an intense desire to light up the world and serve mankind. Electricity yielded its secrets to him, but he paid the price by perseverance, stick-to-itiveness, and confidence, knowing that the answer would come. He gave it attention and devotion. He kept on keeping on, and his deeper mind never failed him.

Self-condemnation and self-criticism are two of the most destructive emotions generating psychic poison throughout your system, robbing you of vitality, strength, and equilibrium, resulting in general debility of the entire organism.

Love is the fulfillment of the law of health, harmony, peace, and abundance. Love means that what you wish for yourself, you must also wish for others. When you love the other person, you're really at peace.

I suggested to a musician that in order to become outstanding in his field, he should pray as follows:

"God is the great musician. I am an instrument and a channel for the divine. The God presence flows through me as harmony, beauty, joy, and peace. The infinite presence and power plays through me the eternal melody of love. When I play, I play the melody of the one who forever is. I am inspired from on high, and majestic cadences come forth, revealing the eternal harmony of God."

Within a few years, he became extraordinarily successful. The price he paid was attention, reverence, and devotion to the eternal being from whom all blessings flow.

A man who cannot make ends meet must pay the price, and the price is not hard labor and burning the midnight oil, but in building into his consciousness the idea of wealth. Man possesses all things by right of consciousness. You can work fourteen or fifteen hours a day, but if your mind is not productive, your labor will be in vain. Is your mind productive?

Wisdom is an awareness of the presence and power of God in you, and understanding is the application of that intelligence and wisdom to solve your daily problems. The Kingdom of God is within you. The kingdom of intelligence, wisdom, power, and beauty, for the divine presence is within you, and all of God is where you are.

You can work fourteen or fifteen hours a day, but if your mind isn't at peace, if you're not full of geniality and cordiality and goodwill, your labor will be in vain, for *"Faith worketh by love."* You may have tremendous faith in your particular field of engineering, science, art, industry, or business, but if you lack cordiality, geniality, and goodwill, you stumble and fall.

The Kingdom of God is there. This means in infinite intelligence, boundless wisdom, and all the power of the infinite are lodged in your deeper mind. God's infinite ideas are available to you if you'd only tune in and rejoice. That infinite spirit is revealing to you what you need to know, for *"God is spirit, and they that worship Him, worship Him in spirit and in truth."*

Worship no man on the face of the earth, for worship is to give your supreme attention, loyalty, and devotion to the one presence and power within you. *"For, I am the Lord. That is my name. My glory you shall not give to another. Neither shall you give my praise. I am, and there is none else, and from the rising of the sun to the setting of the same, there is none else."*

When you realize there's only one power moving as unity and harmony, there is no cause for evil anymore because you've enthroned in your mind the one presence and power.

· · ·

A man who lived near me some years ago told me that back in 1950 he was bankrupt. He prayed for guidance and asked that creative intelligence reveal the next step. He had an overpowering feeling to go into the desert.

While musing there, the idea came to him to visit his father-in-law, who owned some land there. He saw tremendous potentialities he foresaw in that desert place, that people would leave Los Angeles. They'd come out from the East, and they'd build homes and hospitals and schools and all that. His father-in-law hired him as a salesman, promoter of the land.

Today he has his own office and is a multimillionaire in real estate. He was taught from within what to do. He paid the price of recognition, and then following the lead which came to him. The faculty of intuition is within you.

The mere fact that you desire an answer means the answer is already present in the mental and spiritual world in which you live and move and have your being. There's an idea, a principle, an archetype, a pattern, for everything comes out of the invisible. You came out of the invisible yourself, and so did the whole world.

So again, realize that in Him you live and move and have your being. God lives, moves, and has being in you. God is the giver and the gift, and you must be able to receive the gift. You must be a receiver. Many people are very poor receivers. They say, "The good things are not for me. They're for Mrs. Jones down the street, you know."

But everything has been given to you. God Himself indwells you. The whole world is yours. The sun shines on the just and the unjust. The rain falls on the good and the evil. Mathematicians tells us that enough fruit rots in the tropics to feed all humanity, rots in the ground. Go out in the desert and pour out some water. It won't grow anything.

You can have an idea worth a fortune, a creative idea. It will come to you, too, but you must pay the price. Recognize it. You can say,

"Infinite spirit within me reveals better ways in which I can serve. God's creative idea unfolds within me revealing to me new and better ways of accomplishing great things and of serving humanity."

New ideas will come to you, and wonders will happen as you pray that way, but remember you must recognize it is there. You must call upon it. You must have faith in it, it's not mumbo-jumbo.

* * *

Some years ago, I visited Jasper Park Lodge in Alberta, Canada, a very beautiful place. The waitresses and the waiters and the men there are all from the various colleges in Canada. It was summertime, and they're all studying along various lines, but they're all college students.

One of the waitresses there had a very perplexing problem. I suggested to her that at night, prior to sleep, she turn over her request to her deeper mind. I said, "You must recognize it only knows the answer, and go to it with faith and understanding." I said, "When you do, it will respond. You must pay that price. The price is belief and acceptance. Just recognize it is there."

When you turn the tap, you expect the water to flow, don't you? You've paid the price. You believed the water would flow, and then you used your fingers to turn on the tap. She spoke to her deeper mind this way. "Reveal to me the answer. I know that you know only the answer." She lulled herself to sleep with this prayer.

The next day, she received a telegram from Ontario which solved her problem. She had to pay the price by thinking about the answer, knowing it was there. She gave attention to her deeper mind and received the answer in the morning.

The answer will come, but there's something you must do first. *"The Father worketh hither to and I work."* The God presence forever controlling the universe guides the planets in their course, and causes the sun to shine. It's operating in your body, takes care of you when you're sound asleep. You must do something. You must begin to use it.

Call upon it, and it'll respond to you. If you do not call upon it, if you do not recognize it, or if you do not believe in it, it's just the same as if it were not there. For the God presence will do nothing for you except through you, through your own thoughts, your own imagery, your own beliefs and conviction.

You're told, "Get wisdom. In all thy getting, get understanding." A doctor has wisdom, for example. A young intern wanted to become a surgeon, but his hand was shaking, he was nervous. To get rid of that nervousness, he had to take a glass of water full to the brim up and down the stairs without losing a drop. Up the stairs and down again for half an hour everyday.

It took him six months before he had a steady hand. He paid the price. He became a great surgeon, but he had to pay the price: attention and devotion. Up the stairs and down the stairs for half an hour everyday. Would you give up after a while? Would you get bored and say, "I can't be bothered?"

But he wanted to be a surgeon, and he had to pay the price. You don't want the surgeon's hand to shake when you're operating, do you? You want a surgeon who's poised and balanced, serene and calm, and who is skilled and has wisdom.

There's wisdom in the ophthalmologist with a laser beam, where he takes a detached retina and heals it up in a minute or two, or takes out a cataract. He's skilled, because he paid the price of attention. He's called to Arabia. He's called to England, to Ireland, different places. You can rest assured he doesn't have to pray for wealth or money. It just flows through him because he has skill, and he was wisdom.

There's the mechanical wisdom where you can't solve the problem, but the mechanic looks at it, sees it immediately, and solves it. He has studied mechanics, perhaps he loves cars and all their parts, so he gave attention, studied, applied himself, perhaps took a car apart and read up all about the techniques and the modus operandi. Now he's very skilled.

The universal life principle is speaking through you now as a desire, for God speaks to man through desire. You desire to be greater than you are. You desire health, love, peace, harmony, abundance, and security. If you don't, you're abnormal. Your ultimate desire is to have a sense of oneness with God, called the yoga of love.

This life principle will reveal to you the way towards the fulfillment of your dream. It knows how to bring it to pass, but you must open your mind and heart and receive wholeheartedly the gift of the one who forever is. Cast out of your mind all preconceived notions, false beliefs, and superstitions, and realize that, *"Before you call, I will answer. While you're yet speaking, I will hear."*

This means that you must order your mind and your thoughts to conform to the age-old truth that whatever you are seeking already subsists in the infinite mind. It's already there. All you have to do is to identify mentally and emotionally with your desire, idea, plan, or purpose, realizing it is as real as your hand or heart.

For example, you may have a new invention in your mind. You haven't committed it to paper, you haven't drawn a diagram. A good, sensitive psychic or medium or clairvoyant can describe that invention. Why? Because it's already in your mind, and if you're in rapport with the sensitive or the psychic, and they can describe it. Why? It's already there. That's the reality of it.

As you walk the earth in the assumption that your prayer is answered, you shall have the joy of experiencing its reality objectively. The invention on the part of the inventor is as real as its objective counterpart. This is why your desire or new project is also real, subjectively speaking, that new book, that new play. Where is it? It's in your mind. It's real. It has form, shape, and substance in another dimension of mind.

I saw a girl dancing at Jasper Park Lodge. It was easy to see the wisdom, intelligence, order, and rhythm of the spirit flowing through her. She said she was dancing for God, to use her own term. She received tremendous applause for work well done. That's wisdom isn't it? You see the beauty, the order, the symmetry, the proportion, the grace, the charm. All that's wisdom.

She deserved the praise uttered. She danced graciously, gloriously, and rhythmically. She told me that her teacher told her to always pray that God was dancing through her and that God's beauty, order, proportion, and wisdom would always function through her. Struggling, toiling, boiling are not the answer. Reverence for the infinite, contacting the infinite power—that's the answer.

• • •

The late Henry Hamblin of England, the editor of *Science of Thought Review,* told me that he was hard-pressed financially. One day he was walking home in the snow and suddenly became aware that the wealth and love and goodness of God were like the billions of snowflakes falling all around him.

He said, "I opened my mind and heart at the moment to God's infinite riches, knowing that God's wealth, love, and inspiration were falling onto my mind and heart like the snowflakes were falling all over London."

From that moment forward, wealth flowed to him freely, joyously, and endlessly. He never lacked for wealth all the days of his life. He changed his mind, and according to the change in his mind was it done unto him. His environment hadn't changed, London, the snow and fog and everything else. The office was the same. Everything was the same, but he had changed. He had changed internally and become an instrument for the riches of life, spiritually, mentally, in all ways.

There is no such thing as something for nothing. You must always pay the price, and the coin, of course, is attention. Give your attention to music or to electricity or to anything, and love it, and it will give its secrets back to you. Love truth, and say you want to know the inner meaning of the Bible. "I want to know what all these allegories and parables mean."

If you have a hunger and thirst, all the inner meanings will be given to you. Whether given to you from within like Quimby, or through a teacher, what difference does it make? For all wisdom is within you. Wisdom will be transmitted to you as you realize that the infinite is within you.

In the case of Vera Radcliffe, our organist, men and women pay her with money, and also in praise. She's invited here, there, and everywhere. She can't accept all the invitations because there are too many. She loves music and knows a lot about it, has practiced it and given attention to it and paid the price. Wisdom is the principle thing. Wisdom is the presence and power of God functioning in you. "With all thy getting," you're told, "get understanding."

"In all thy ways acknowledge Him, and he will plain thy paths. Trust Him and believe in Him, and he will bring it to pass."

●   ●   ●

Here's another example of a woman who paid the price. I read it in the *Times,* May the 2nd, 1975. The headline says, "In the Driver's Seat," and the photo is captioned, "Maude is still wheeling and dealing at age 103." This is what he said:

> "She peers out from behind her Coke bottle glasses walking in small, slow steps toward her pride and joy. For most people her age, pride and joy would mean great-grandchildren or maybe

even great-great-grandchildren, but for 103-year-old Maude Towle, the greatest thing in her life is her car.

"Despite the fact that she is 38 years past retirement age, she recently passed the test for renewal of her California driver's license for the 11th straight year. Maude Towle is one of the 10 oldest drivers in the state, but that is just part of her story. As spry at 103 as most are at 65, she handles payments for a home mortgage company seven days a week.

"'I'll never retire,' she said, 'because if I ever did, I'd starve. They just don't pay enough with Social Security for even an old person like me to eat these days. This way, I never have to apologize to anyone. I can live the way I want and do the things I want without always being told what to do.'

"Mrs. Towle lives in an Englewood apartment house. Her best friend and constant companion, Ida Gleason, lives in a nearby apartment. Mrs. Gleason is another spring chicken. She's only 93. They ride in the crowded streets of Englewood every day, bound for the market, the bank, or the local park where they love to spend their time playing cards under a shady tree.

"Mrs. Towle began driving in 1965 after her husband died. Since then, it has been she and Ida Gleason on their own. Mrs. Towle said she wouldn't have it any other way. 'I don't take any favors,' she said, 'I earn everything I get. I've always made my own way, and I always will.'

"But most of all, Mrs. Towle loves her car, a shiny, brown and white electric two-seater. It only goes 20 miles an hour, but somehow it seems much faster. She carefully rolls back the cover that has kept the paint job looking new for four years. This task takes about 10 minutes. Then she's ready to unlock the doors. Again, the utmost care is used to make sure the paint isn't scratched. Finally, she climbs in, and Mrs. Gleason sits beside her. With a gentle whirring sound, Mrs. Towle and Mrs. Gleason are off for another busy day."

She has a love of life, she paid the price, she loves life, she's interested in life. She's not interested in a handout or things of that nature. She's interested in contributing to humanity and has a great love for life that will show her the path. Serenity, tranquility, humor, and laughter keep you young.

Patience never grows old. Love never grows old. Joy never grows old. Harmony never grows old. Laughter never grows old. Goodwill never grows old. Gentleness and kindness never grow old, nor compassion or understanding. These are eternal.

The life principle never grows old, either. It was never born, it will never die. *"Water wets it not, fire burns it not, and wind blows it not away."* So, that life principle in you is eternal. We grow old when we are bitter, when we are resentful, hateful, when we're full of self-condemnation and ill will. These emotions and thoughts corrode our soul, and we grow old regardless of our age chronologically.

Here's a man who paid a price. He had a hunger and thirst, and a great interest, too. A vision gave an inventor an idea that changed the world. This was published in a newspaper some time ago. I'm quoting now:

"The man who invented the steam engine forever changed the world, got his ideas from a vision. 'The engine was given to me from the outside,' James Watt said. 'I did not create it. I only accepted it.' Watt was born in Scotland, 1736, had little formal education. He earned his living as a repairman in Glasgow. 'I could repair nearly every kind of mechanical device,' Watt once said.

"'One day in 1764, a customer brought a defective engine into my shop. This one event was to change my life completely. A Newcomen engine was a very crude steam engine. It was occasionally used in mines to pump out water, but it was never very efficient, consuming a lot of energy and accomplishing very little work.'

"While Watt was fixing the engine, he conceived the idea of an entirely new kind of steam engine that would overcome all the faults of the Newcomen, but he lacked the knowledge to convert his idea into reality. Then, a vision came to him one Sunday afternoon in May 1766 while he was walking in a Glasgow park thinking and dwelling upon the engine. The vision: Watt said he saw a steam engine in complete detail. 'Before I had walked much further, the whole thing was arranged in my mind.'

"The next morning he went to work, and in less than 12 hours, he had built a new engine that efficiently harnessed the power of steam. He patented the idea in 1781, and in 1782 won additional patents for improvements. There have been few changes in it since 1782.

"Watt's invention was soon put to work in factories replacing animals and men and triggering the start of the industrial revolution."

That's why I say you can have an idea worth a fortune. You can have an idea putting millions to work. James Watt paid the price. The coin that he paid was attention, interest, and devotion, realizing that he could bring forth an engine that would serve humanity.

Here's a story of another man who paid a price, written by Bill Benovsky, called, "Try and Try Again." It was in the *Herald Examiner*, April 17, 1975. Of course there's nothing new about it, you read it in your history. However it's interesting to show how you must pay the price.

"There are a number of qualities which contribute to personal success in life. Some, like being born with good parents or in a favorable country or social class, or with natural physical and mental endowments, are completely out of our control, but the ones that really count are the ones that we can do something about, and among these nothing is so important as the quality of persistence.

"You may pick at random from a library shelf the biography of any man or woman who has made a lasting contribution to humanity. Some were extremely brilliant. Others showed uncommon persistence. Let's take the case of Albert Einstein. In grade school, he was such an unimpressive student that when his father asked the headmaster what profession young Albert should pursue, the headmaster replied, 'It really doesn't matter because he will never make a success at anything.' Einstein became one of the premier intellectuals of the 20th century and probably the greatest physicist of all time, more by reason of determined persistence than because of easy genius.

"Many similar cases can be cited. We're celebrating the 100th year of Winston Churchill. In school, he was a very slow student. As a public servant, his career was thought to be rather dull in the 1930s, and he had failed to achieve most of his dreams and goals, but by staying alert and alive, he was prepared when the rare opportunity for leadership came at age 66. At a time when most men are retired, he became in 1941 the British prime minister and rallied, not only his own countrymen, but all the Western world. Because of his bulldog tenacity, he came to be regarded as the greatest political leader of the 20th century."

He paid the price, didn't he? Attention, devotion, loyalty, yes, persistence, stick-to-itiveness, refusing to take no for an answer, always realizing that there was a power that responded.

"The story of America's greatest statesman is likewise not a story of easy success, but one of dogged persistence. He failed at business in 1831, was defeated for the state legislature in 1833. He was elected to the state legislature in 1834. His sweetheart died in 1835. He had a nervous breakdown in 1836. He was defeated for speaker in 1838. He was defeated for elector in 1840. He was defeated for Congress in 1843.

"Finally, he was elected for one term in Congress in 1846 only to be defeated again for Congress in 1848. He was defeated for the Senate in 1855, was defeated for vice president in 1856, and was defeated again for the Senate in 1858. Finally, in 1860, he was elected president of the United States. There were just a few rough spots in the life of Abraham Lincoln.

"Franklin Roosevelt, who was president of the United States longer than any other man, was severely crippled by polio and served all of those years of the Depression and war in a wheelchair. One of his great strengths was a powerful use of public speaking, especially at a time when the radio had given direct access to all the American population.

"These famous fireside chats sounded informal and off the cuff, but in Hyde Park, New York, is a glass case displaying nine drafts of one of Roosevelt's famous speeches. The first was rough, the second improved, the third shows still greater improvement, and in the eighth draft, only one word had to be changed before the ninth and final draft was run. 'Trifle,' said Michelangelo, 'makes perfection, for perfection itself is not trifle.'"

I heard many of these fireside chats, and you perhaps thought he was talking off the cuff. Think of the hours, perhaps days, it took for all those experts to gather together all the data and information, and then the speech is put together and he goes over it again and again and again. That's perfection, isn't it? Perfection is not a trifle. Those talks were very effective and had a tremendous influence.

Churchill was also a spellbinder who appeared to speak completely extemporaneously. But as one of his biographers correctly noted, "Sir Winston Churchill spent most of his life working on his 'impromptu' speeches."

I heard him talk one time, and you'd think he was talking off the cuff, but there were days and weeks behind it. He would pace the floor and talk to himself for hours, perfecting it.

Press on. Nothing in the world can take the place of persistence. Talent will not—nothing is more common than unsuccessful men with talent. Genius will not. Unrewarded genius is almost a proverb. Education alone will not. The world is full of educated derelicts. Persistence and determination alone are omnipotent.

"Try and Try Again" reminds you of some history which I'm sure you've read about in school, but it's good to be reminded that they paid the price, too. Persistence, stick-to-itiveness, determination, attention—for attention is the key to life. It's the key to success.

*   *   *

"If thine eye be single, thy whole body is full of light." The *Eye* is spiritual perception. It's spiritual awareness, and you must put this God presence first in your life and realize supreme and omnipotent is the only presence, power, cause, and substance. Give all honor, allegiance, and devotion to that, and realize it's your guide, your counselor, your way-shower, your troubleshooter, your adjuster, your Father, your pain master, and the source of all blessings. There is no other power. Think of the wonders that will happen in your life as you give attention to that great truth.

Give your attention to it, your devotion to it, your loyalty to it. Not to stones and created things, men and women, or the weather—look at the many gods you have. One condition doesn't create another. One circumstance doesn't create another.

To give attention to created things means you're not willing to pay the price, as the price is the one power, the one presence, the one cause, and the one substance. There is none else. That's the great illumination, that's the final word. When you awaken to that, then, and only then, are you a truth student.

Be honest with yourself, and ask yourself this question: "Do I really believe in my heart that there's only one presence as the living spirit within me? It's omnipotent, omnipresent, omni-action. It's all there is. It's the very ground I'm walking on. Do I give any power to the phenomenalistic world, or any created thing? Do I give power to stars, to the sun and the moon, the weather, men and women, sticks and stones, karma, or past lives, voodoo or devils?"

There aren't any such things. There's no room for any devil. *"In all, over all, through all, all in all, I Am and there is none else. From the rising of the sun, to the setting of the same, there is none else."* Are you willing to pay that price?

You must pay that price, and then count your illumine. Then you are free because, *"From the rising of the sun to the setting of the same, there is none else. I am the Lord. That is my name. My glory you shall not give to another. Neither shall you give my praise."*

"I am the Lord. That is my name." I Am is being life awareness. There is none else. There's only the one presence and the one power, the one cause, and the

one substance. Be wonderful when you come to that conclusion, the definite conclusion.

Suggestion is a power if you accept, but it's not the power. The power is the one power moving as unity, no divisions or quarrels in it. How could spirit fight itself? How could one part of spirit fight another part of spirit in any part of the world?

That's the greatest of all truths, and, *"The Lord thy God is a jealous God, jealous in the sense you mustn't know another."* Not jealous from a human standpoint. The minute you give power to any other created thing, at that moment your mind is divided. You're the double-minded man, unstable in all your ways.

"Let not such a man ask anything of God, for he is like the surge of the sea tossed to and fro, double-minded man, unstable in all his ways." You're like the woman I said earlier was blaming the climate in Denver, genes and chromosomes, blaming it on everything, while the cause was within herself all the time. She learned to pay the price and got a healing.

Lee Harrison wrote this in the *Inquirer*, with the headline "Medicine Failed Me, Then I Was Cured By the Miracle of Prayer":

"Dr. Phil Miles once was skeptical about supernatural healing, but no more. For when a bizarre disease attacked his body, gnarling and paralyzing his limbs, it was faith, not modern medicine, that cured him. 'It was a miracle,' declared the El Paso, Texas, physician. Joy shining in his eyes, 'It's given me,' he said, 'new life. I'm walking, living, laughing proof that there's a healing force much more powerful than any man on this earth.'

"For seven years Dr. Miles had suffered from this strange disease which caused his arms and legs to jerk spasmodically and twist into rigid positions. Dr. Miles, formerly on the staff of the prestigious Walter Reed Medical Center, called in some of the finest neurologists in America, but they couldn't even diagnose his illness.

"Finally bedridden and growing worse every hour, the heartsick young doctor turned in desperation to his only remaining hope, faith—faith in God. He asked a Christian neighbor to come to his beside, help him pray for his recovery.

"The doctor will never forget that incredible day. Every moment, every happening, is etched into his memory. 'I was sobbing uncontrollably as I uttered the words of that prayer,' he recalled. 'No sooner had the final words left my lips when to my utter astonishment, my hands, which had been clenched like claws for two days suddenly began to open. A second later, the rigid muscles in my feet began to relax. I realized I was witnessing the power of the supernatural. Within two days,' he said, 'he was back on his feet.'

"Today, more than two years later, he's still healthy, and working again as a specialist in obstetrics and gynecology at William Beaumont Army Medical Center in El Paso, Texas. Dr. Miles, 36 years of age, said the unknown disease struck him without warning in 1965. 'I was examined by some of the best neurologists in the country, but they couldn't positively diagnose my illness. In my heart, I knew I had a form of multiple sclerosis.'"

Here is a man who paid the price. He tried everything before he surrendered to the God presence, which made him, which created him, which knows all things. He prayed the fervent, effectual prayer of righteous man. He called in a neighbor. They prayed together, a humble prayer, but a complete surrender recognizing the great truth in his heart.

Sobbing while he prayed—there's nothing wrong with that. It means humility. It means a complete surrender, turning the whole thing over to that which is, which knows all and sees all. For the Bible says, "*I am the Lord that healeth thee. I am the Lord thy God. I will come and heal thee. I will restore health into thee and heal thee of thy wounds, sayeth the Lord.*"

Who healeth all the disease? Who satisfieth thy mouth with good things? Who restoreth thy youth like the eagle? Are you going to say it is hard for me? Is the Lord's hand shortened that he cannot save?

You must realize that every man has to pay the price, and that price is attention, recognition, acceptance, and conviction. You can pay the price, too. All you have to do is call upon it. It answers you. It's impersonal, no respecter of persons.

Let us dwell upon these great truths.

"But my God shall supply all you need according to his riches and glory."

"In quietness and in confidence shall be your strength."

"God who giveth us richly all things to enjoy, but with God, all things are possible."

"Before they call, I will answer; while they're yet speaking, I will hear."

"According to your faith, be it unto you."

"If thou can believe, all things are possible to him that believeth."

"He shall call upon me, and I will answer him. I will be with him in trouble. I will deliver him and honor him."

"The Lord is my light and my salvation. Whom shall I fear? The Lord is a strength in my life. Of whom shall I be afraid?"

"God in the midst of you is guiding you now."

Your Friend the Subconscious

There is one mind common to all individual men. There are two spheres of activity within one mind. There are not two minds. Your conscious mind is the reasoning mind, that phase of mind which chooses, weighs, dissects, analyzes, investigates, scrutinizes, comes to conclusions and decisions.

For example, you choose your books, your home, your partner in life. You make all your decisions with your conscious mind. On the other hand, without any conscious choice on your part, your heart just keeps functioning automatically, and the process of digestion, circulation, and breathing are carried on by your subconscious mind through processes independent of your conscious control.

Your subconscious mind accepts what is impressed upon it or what you consciously believe. It does not reason out things like your conscious mind. It's a one-track mind, it doesn't argue with you controversially.

Your subconscious mind is like the soil which accepts any kind of idea, good or bad. Your thoughts are active and might be likened unto seeds. Negative, destructive thoughts continue to work negatively in your subconscious mind, and in due time will come forth into outer experience, which corresponds with them.

Remember, your subconscious mind does not engage in proving whether your thoughts are good or bad, true or false, but responds according to the nature of your thoughts or suggestions. For example, if you consciously assume something to be true even though it may be false, your subconscious mind will accept it as true and proceed to bring about results which must necessarily follow—because you consciously assumed it to be true.

Your subconscious mind cannot argue controversially. Hence if you give it wrong suggestions, it will accept them as true and will proceed to bring them to pass as conditions, experiences, and events. Your subconscious mind is oftentimes referred to as your subjective mind. Your subjective mind takes cognizance of its environment by means independent of the five senses.

Your subjective mind perceives by intuition. It is the seat of your emotions and the storehouse of memory. Your subjective mind performs its highest functions when your objective senses are in abeyance. It is that intelligence which makes itself manifest when the objective mind is suspended or in a sleepy, drowsy state.

Your subjective mind sees without the use of the natural organs of vision. It has the capacity of clairvoyance and clairaudience. Your subjective mind can leave your body, travel to distant lands, and bring back information oft times of the most exact and truthful character.

Through your subjective mind, you can read the thoughts of others, read the contents of sealed envelopes and closed safes. Your subjective mind has the ability to apprehend the thoughts of others without the use of the ordinary, objective means of communication. It is of the greatest importance that we understand the interaction of your objective and subjective mind in order to learn the true art of prayer.

When your conscious and subconscious mind function harmoniously and peacefully, when they work together in unison and in harmony, the result of that is harmony, health, peace and joy and happiness. All the evil, pain, suffering, misery, war, crime, and sickness in the world are due to the inharmonious relationship of your conscious and subconscious mind.

Remember we said your subconscious is impersonal and non-selective. In the Bible, it says, *"The husband is head of the wife."* The husband in the Bible is your conscious mind, and the wife is the subconscious. That's not true from a literal standpoint, but it's true psychologically.

Your subconscious is controlled by your conscious mind. It's amenable to suggestion and controlled by it. The wife, your subconscious, is subject to the man, the conscious mind, in all things. That's only true psychologically.

Whatever your conscious mind feels to be true, your subconscious accepts. Your capacity to imagine and feel, and your freedom to choose the idea you want to entertain, gives you power over all creation.

Do not dwell on the imperfections and shortcomings of others, or their frailties or derelictions. Why? Because whatever you think and feel about another, you create in your own mind, body, and circumstances. Ask yourself, "Would I like to live with what I'm thinking and wishing for the other?" If you would, you're on the right track.

Your thought is creative, and what you think about the other, you are creating in your pocketbook too, and in all phases of your life. What you do not wish done unto you, do not feel it is done unto you or another.

Chance or accident is not responsible for the things that happen to you, nor is predestined faith, the author of fortune or misfortune. Your subconscious mind is not concerned with the truth or falseness of what you consciously feel or believe to be true. Select only that which is true, lovely, noble, and Godlike, and your subconscious will reproduce accordingly.

The Bible says, *"Believe you have it now, and you shall receive it. All things whatsoever you shall ask in prayer, believe that you have it now, and you shall receive it."* That's a psychological law. Assume the mood that would be yours had you realized your desire, and as you do this, wonders will begin to happen in your life.

* * *

Edison discovered, or he knew intuitively, that the voice caused undulatory currents in the atmosphere. He reasoned it out, believing such currents could reproduce the voice. The idea came to him where in as much as your voice produces waves, these waves will reproduce that voice. That's believing you have it now, and you shall receive it.

So he developed a phonograph, and the idea came from his subconscious mind. Your subconscious is your friend. It seeks to heal you, to restore you. If someone is presenting you with a phony deal, there's something within you that warns you. That's your subconscious mind prompting you. Its intimations, urgings, promptings, murmurings are always lifeward. It seeks to heal you if you cut yourself. If you burn yourself, it seeks to reduce the edema. It gives you new skin and tissue.

If your child is very sick, and you're completely exhausted, think about waking up to give the medicine to your child at 2:00 or 3:00 in the morning and it will wake you up, no matter how tired you are, to minister to your child.

Its tendency is always lifeward. Electricity, Edison knew, was produced by friction. Reverse it—electricity, in turn, produces friction. Edison knew the transformation of forces, and he knew that the force is reversible. Heat produces mechanical motion; mechanical motion produces heat.

Cause and effect, action and reaction. These are cosmic and universal. Pray believing that you already possess what you pray for. Yes, it will come to pass. This is the law of inverse transformation.

For example, if the sale of your home brought a certain amount of joy, satisfaction, and elation into your mental atmosphere, then the feeling that would be yours if you realized it would also produce that. In other words, that feeling or that mental state captured in your imagination and feeling must produce the sale of the home. If the actual sale of the home brought a certain joy and satisfaction to you, then reverse it.

Capture the feeling, the mood that would be yours if you sold it, by imagining the check in your hand, giving thanks for it, depositing it into the bank. Do the things you would do if your home sold, all in your mind or your imagination, and that attitude of mind will produce it. Awaken within yourself the feeling that would be yours if you realized your desire now, and that feeling will produce it.

A young boy, a DeMolay boy who wanted to go to a certain college, had difficulty and was rejected. I said to him, "You understand this law of inverse transformation. How would you feel if they accepted you now? If you went in to see this man who rejected you, and he said, 'We've changed our minds. We've looked over your qualifications and you are accepted.'"

He said, "I'd feel happy. I'd call up my dad and tell him. I'd feel wonderful."

"Well," I said, "as you go to sleep at night, feel that I'm congratulating your acceptance and your marvelous success in the college. Imagine you're also talking to your dad and telling him you've been accepted. You're going there now in your own mind. It's wonderful. You can capture that feeling in your imagination, that inner mood." He did that, and he was accepted.

The feeling of the answered prayer, if assumed and sustained, must objectify the answer to your prayer. That's the meaning of *"He calleth things that be not as though they were, and the unseen become seen."* If a physical fact can produce a psychological state, then that psychological state can produce a physical fact. That's the meaning of, *"All things whatsoever you shall ask in prayer, believe that you have it now, and you shall receive it."*

How can you believe you have it now when the reality of it is an idea, a mental picture in your mind? You accept the mental picture, dramatize it, feel the reality of it, rejoice in it. Believe in the law of growth knowing that the seed you put in the ground will grow if you nourish it, sustain it, water it, and fertilize it.

"The philosophy of 6,000 years has not searched the chambers and the magazines of the soul," Emerson said. Your consciousness is the sum total of all your subjective and objective impressions and awareness. Your mind is a medium of ideas, a collection of impressions. Some are good, and perhaps some are not so bad. Your mind is therefore a medium for all sorts of impressions, and your mind should be open only to ideas which heal, bless, inspire, elevate, and dignify your soul, for ideas are our masters. Ideas generate emotions.

The reason there is so much misery in the world is the ideas many men hold are completely false. These emotions get snarled up in the subconscious and they must have an outlet. Being of a negative nature, it must be a negative outlet.

James Watt was a Scotsman, a mechanic. His mother was making a cup of tea, and he saw the result of the steam forcing the lid up. He began to think what would happen if he harnessed that steam—tremendous power there. The idea came from his subconscious mind to force steam into a cylinder which contained a piston. The expansion forced the piston back and drove the wheels. That was the beginning of the steam engine, which revolutionized industry all over the world.

When a man says it can't be done because it was never done before, it's impossible, remember the science of aerodynamics states that a bumblebee cannot fly because its wingspan is too short, and its weight is too great. But the bumblebee doesn't know what's in the textbook, so it goes ahead and flies.

So when someone says it can't be done, the man who knows the power of his imagination of the great friend within him says, "I'm going to do it. It can be done." And the subconscious, which is his friend, responds to him and brings it to pass in a wonderful way.

●   ●   ●

Someone mailed me a clipping from the Copley News Service. A Mexican man was praying for wealth, that is, he wanted money to do the things he wanted to do. According to the article he was poor, and he had gone to Guadalupe to pray. In a dream he saw the Virgin, and she said to him in the dream, "Purchase this ticket, 37281, in the Mexican Lottery."

He called his nephew in Texas and asked him to track it down, so the nephew tracked it down, and he invested the uncle's money to buy a block of tickets. The uncle won $3 million, the grand prize in Mexico.

Then the Internal Revenue Service visited his nephew and said, "We want $1,600,000 because you're here in America and you bought this ticket." So he took it to the tax court, and the judge said, "This man received an answer to his prayer from the Virgin, and the ticket was purchased in his name, and the Internal Revenue doesn't get anything."

That's the friend who gave $3 million to this Mexican, who believed that the Virgin would answer him. That's the friend that's within you. Its ways are past finding out.

Of course the Virgin is the *I Am* within you, your own subconscious mind. It's capable of infinite conceptions within itself. That's why Mary means "the sea." *Virgin* means of pure mind, the infinite mind, the I Am, the presence of God within you. That's called the Virgin Mary in all Bibles of the world. Mary is a Latin word meaning the sea.

It has nothing at all to do with a woman or a virgin or anything of that nature because what's within you is capable of an infinite number of conceptions of itself, without the aid of any man. It created a whole universe.

For example, the tree outside your door is an immaculate conception. So is the whole universe an immaculate conception. It came out of the mind of God. He had no one to aid Him, for God is all there is, and therefore only God can make a tree.

That's the Virgin that is within you. Even though he had blind faith and thought he was praying to a Virgin, his subconscious responded because your subconscious responds whether the object of your faith be true or false. That's a very interesting thing to know. It'll answer to blind belief, too.

In the subconscious mind, there is an intelligence and wisdom which provides aid in emergencies when a direct demand is made upon it. There are many, many such instances where scientists have received answers to their prayers, when they couldn't get an answer any other way.

Nikola Tesla was a brilliant electrical scientist who brought forth the most amazing innovations. He said when an idea for a new invention came into his mind, he would build it up in his imagination, knowing that his subconscious mind would reconstruct and reveal to his conscious mind all the parts needed for its manufacture in concrete form.

Through quietly contemplating every possible improvement, he spent no time in correcting defects and was able to give the technicians the perfect product of his mind. He said, "Invariably my device works, as I imagined it should. In twenty years there has not been a single exception." His subconscious mind gave him the answer to all his inventions.

A famous chemist, Friedrich von Stradonitz, used his subconscious mind to solve his problem as follows: For a long time he had been trying to rearrange the sixth carbon and sixth hydrogen atoms of the benzene formula. He was constantly perplexed and unable to solve the matter.

Tired and exhausted, he turned the request over completely to his subconscious mind. Shortly afterward, he was about to board a London bus. His subconscious presented his conscious mind with a sudden flash of a snake biting its own tail and turning around like a pinwheel.

This answer from his subconscious mind gave him the long-sought answer, the circular rearrangement of the atoms that is known as the benzene ring. Every high school boy knows how that came to pass through this flash of illumination from the depths of the man's subconscious mind. Countless inventions come through that way.

The Bible says, *"I the Lord,"* meaning your subconscious mind, *"will make myself known to man in a vision, will speak to man in a dream."* When I use the term "subconscious mind," I'm talking about the great universal mind. I'm not looking at it from a Freudian, narrow standpoint where it deals with sexual repressions, frustrations, and inhibitions—not at all.

I'm talking of the father within which does the work. You can call it the supernormal mind, a superconscious mind, the subliminal mind. You can call it Allah, Brahma, reality, infinite intelligence, self-originating spirit, life principle. Call it by any name you want; it's nameless anyhow, but it's that subjective wisdom and intelligence that controls all your vital organs when you're sound asleep, that sometimes answers your prayer in a dream, a vision of the night.

There are numerous references in the Bible to dreams, visions, revelations, and warnings given to men during sleep. Your subconscious mind is active 24 hours a day, it's your greatest friend. The Bible points out that Joseph was accurate in his analysis of the dreams of Pharaoh. His mental acumen and sagacity in predicting the future through the interpretation of dreams bought him praise, honor, and recognition from the king.

Dreams have captivated scientists, scholars, mystics, and philosophers down through the ages. Many answers to man's most acute problems have been given in dreams. Since Biblical days, various interpreters and expositors in every country have been engaged in the analysis and interpretation of dreams.

Freud, Jung, Adler, and many other distinguished psychologists and psychiatrists have studied the symbols portrayed in dreams, and by interpreting the meaning to the conscious mind of the patient, they have released hidden phobias, fixations, and other mental complexes.

Your dreams, of course, are projections of the contents of your subconscious mind. In many instances they answer your problems and warn you regarding investments, journeys, and marriage as well as pitfalls of daily living.

Your dream is a dramatization of your subconscious mind. It is not fatalistic. You mold, fashion, and shape your own destiny by your thought and feeling. Anything in your subconscious mind is subject to change, and when you know the laws of mind you predict your own future. You can fill your subconscious mind with the truth of God, and you will crowd out from your mind everything unlike God.

For the lower is subject to the higher. Your subconscious is subject to the conscious mind. That's the husband, who has charge over the wife in Biblical language. Theologians have taken that literally for thousands of years and have held women in bondage, enthralled them in subjection due to a misinterpretation of the scripture.

* * *

Once I had a telephone call from a woman in New York City, stating that her husband had told her prior to his transition that he planned to take a large sum of money from his private safe and invest it in a foreign country for greater returns.

He passed on a few days later and when the safe deposit in the bank was open, there was no cash. However there was a record at the bank that he had visited the vault two days previously. There was no trace or record of any investment, and an inspection of his desk revealed no clues.

I suggested she turn her request over to her subconscious mind, which knew the answer, for it knows only the answer, and that it would reveal the answer to her in its own way. She prayed as follows:

> "My subconscious mind knows where my husband secreted that money, and I accept the answer and believe implicitly the solution will come clearly into my conscious mind."

She quietly dwelled on the meaning of these words, knowing they would be impressed in her subconscious mind and thereby activating its response.

She had a very vivid dream in which she saw a small, black box hidden behind a picture of Lincoln on the wall in her husband's work den. She was shown in the dream how to press the secret button which could not be seen with the naked eye. When she awakened, she rushed to the den and took down the picture of Lincoln. When she pressed the button revealed in the dream, an opening appeared containing the black box which contained $50,000 in currency.

She discovered the treasures of her subconscious. She discovered there was a friend within her which knows all, sees all, and has the know-how of accomplishment because it is all wise. You too can take a similar step in putting the wisdom of your subconscious to pass, to answer your prayer.

A young woman in San Francisco experienced a recurring dream for four consecutive nights. Her fiancé, who was living in Los Angeles, appeared to her in the dreams and quite suddenly a very high mountain came between them, which seemed impossible to scale. She was deeply surprised, frustrated, and bewildered.

She awoke wrestling with the problem and sensing something very wrong. I asked her what the mountain signified to her, as every dream when interpreted properly must coincide with the inner awareness and feeling of the dreamer. Moreover, a recurrent dream is very important, as it is the intuitive voice of your subconscious saying to you, "Stop, look, and listen."

The word "mountain" to her meant an insuperable obstacle. I suggested she speak to her fiancé about the dream and gain the assurance that there was nothing hidden that was not revealed, nothing covered up that was not made known to her.

Accordingly, she flew down to Los Angeles to see her fiancé, who met her at the airport. After a heart-to-heart talk, he finally told her, "I am a homosexual. I wanted to marry you so that my customers, who are very religious, would not suspect anything." Her dream prevented her from experiencing what eventually would have been a great, traumatic shock.

You too can exercise the same or greater foresight through analyzing the recurrent happenings in your dream. Of course there are variegated dreams, some due to sexual frustration or repression. Others are due to mental and emotional turmoil, bodily malfunctioning, fears, and religious taboos, reproduction and a recast of past events or the activities of the day.

However there are many dreams of a recurring nature as well that are of a precognitive significance, wherein you see events before they happen. Many times you're given detailed instructions as to what action to take.

There is a wonderful power within you, a subconscious intelligence and wisdom that man can use. He may be religious. He may be agnostic. He may be an atheist, and yet he can experience this infinite intelligence and wisdom functioning for him, because you need no creed. It will answer you just as well as it will the atheist or the agnostic, if you call upon it.

It's impersonal, no respecter of persons. You can call it a superhuman intelligence if you want to, or a subliminal mind or subjective mind, or the I Am. They call it Om in India, but the point is the presence of the infinite is within you. It's in your own subliminal depths. It's also a law.

It is there, and we should use it. It works as you sleep. A German proverb says, "Night brings counsel." You know, your body doesn't rest. Your heart and all the vital organs are working while you're sound asleep. Your conscious mind is in abeyance.

You're turned away from the vexation and the strife and the contentions of the day, but two-thirds of your life is controlled by the one-third you spend in sleep. What do you go to sleep with every night? Go to sleep in the feeling that you're a tremendous success, that you're absolutely outstanding. If you have a problem, contemplate the solution. Say, "Infinite intelligence gives me the solution. I accept the answer. It comes to me in divine order."

That subjective self of you corrects the errors of the day and anchors your thought to the supreme intelligence within you. In other words, the ancient Hebrews said, "*You participate in the wisdom and the fore-knowledge of the gods when you're sound asleep,*" because healing currents are released when you're asleep.

The Bible says, "*He giveth His beloved in sleep. I lay me down in peace to sleep for thou Lord maketh me dwell in safety.*"

• • •

Arthur Rohr is a great industrialist and business tycoon. When he has a conference and there's a very important decision to be made, he closes his eyes, relaxes, lets go, and his associates do the same thing. They get quiet and still. What do you suppose they're thinking about?

There's an infinite intelligence within them that knows the answer, knows what's best for the organization, for there's nothing it doesn't know. Therefore they contemplate that right decision, the harmonious solution, the creative idea, in the quietness of their own mind.

In that quietude, that relaxed state when the conscious mind is in abeyance, the wisdom of the subconscious rises to the conscious mind and he gets marvelous results. When they open their eyes they know the decision to make, and it's always right because when your motivation is right, your decision will be right. If your motivation is wrong, no matter what you do, it will be wrong.

When you're asked to make a decision, ask yourself, "What is my motivation? It looks good to me, and that proposition he made looks sound. I prayed about it. Infinite intelligence guides me, directs me what to do, and reveals to me the answer." Then, it looks good to you, and your motivation is right, and whatever you do will be right because it will be right action for you.

Robert Coleman who used to be an usher here, is now living in Albuquerque, New Mexico. He's familiar with a number of Native American medicine men down there. He told me an interesting thing about a member of the tribe who was very ill, and the medicine men couldn't do anything for her.

They brought in this special medicine man, and he said when he came in, they had a pot of boiling water. The test of a medicine man is that he can put his hands or arm into this boiling water, leave it there for about 10 minutes, and there will be no inflammation, no burn of any kind. That's a sure sign he has served his apprenticeship and is disciplined and trained.

After that he put some blankets on the woman, chanted some Indian songs—that is, prayers and incantations based upon their tribal beliefs. He lay down beside the woman, and went to sleep calling on the Great Spirit. And when he woke up, the friend had healed her. The friend, of course, meant the Great Spirit. That's what this particular tribe calls God, "the Great Spirit."

What did he mean by that? He came believing, and in this passive, quiet state of mind, as he began to chant, the woman was receptive, open-minded, and ready to receive. *"According to your faith, is it done unto you. According to your belief, is it done unto you."* The medicine man was full of faith and confidence in the vitality, intelligence, and the miraculous healing power that is within him. Thus in that deeper state of mind his faith was communicated to her, and she got well.

That's what we call prayer therapy. Some people call it spiritual treatment, and so forth. It's simply dwelling upon the infinite spirit and power that is within you. *"I am the Lord that healeth thee. I am the Lord, thy God. I will come and heal thee. I will restore health unto thee and heal thee of they wounds, sayeth the Lord."*

All healing is of the most high, but there's only one healing presence, and when you pray for a person just like this medicine man did, you don't dwell on symptoms or the bodily condition, such as a fever. You dwell upon the intelligence, the wisdom, the vitality, the wholeness and the beauty, and the perfection of the infinite that is animating, sustaining, and strengthening this other person. Then the presence of God is resurrected in the other. That's the basis of all healing.

. . .

Dr. Elsie McCoy in Beverly Hills wrote an article for my book *Psychic Perception*. She has studied extensively in Europe and in Asia, and she shows clearly what construction thinking, according to principle, will accomplish.

Ever since she was eighteen years old, she has made it a habit, she said, to affirm during the day, "Only divine right action takes place in my life," she says. "Whatever I need to know is revealed to me instantly by the infinite intelligence within me." Her gradual reiteration of these truths caused them to reach the subconscious mind, which responded accordingly.

In her early days she was engaged to a prominent surgeon in Chicago. They were separated by over 1,000 miles due to their different assignments. One night while she was sound asleep, she saw and heard clearly in a vivid dream her fiancé in Chicago talking to a nurse. In addition dating her for a weekend, he said to her, "You know I'm engaged, but she is 1,000 miles away and knows nothing about this."

Dr. McCoy phoned him the next day and told him about the silly and foolish dream she'd had and laughed about it. He was furious and accused her of having employed detectives and of spying on him. With that, she dissolved the engagement, and subsequent events showed the wisdom of her subconscious in protecting her from what would have undoubtedly been a tragic marriage.

Her right thinking activated her subconscious mind, which revealed to her what she needed to know before she got married. That's a very interesting thing. The subjective seeks to protect you if only you'll listen to it. While some brush these things aside and say, "Oh, it's only a dream."

There's such a thing as precognition, or prescience, seeing events before they happen. You can protect yourself if you see something negative for yourself or another, because prayer will change your mind.

Also in *Psychic Perception*, I wrote about a girl named Louise Barrows, before she got married. She's now Mrs. Wright, a secretary of mine. She was informed many years ago by a surgeon that it was necessary to operate on her left foot, and that this would necessitate having her leg in a cast as well as using crutches for two months or more.

She prayed that infinite intelligence of subconscious mind would guide and direct her to come to the right decision. Every night she turned this request over to her subconscious mind. At the end of a fortnight she saw a doctor, a friend of the family, who in the dream state pointed to hexagram thirty-five in the *I Ching*, which said, "Progress."

The next day she went to visit him, and on examining the foot, he advised her that he could bring about a perfect alignment and adjustment by manipulation and exercise, which she would have to practice. A perfect healing followed.

That was back in 1961, the first time I gave a series of lectures on the meaning of the *I Ching* for Southern California. I believe I was the first to introduce it here.

The subconscious mind usually speaks and reveals answers symbolically. Louise, having taken two classes on the *I Ching* with the speaker, became absorbed and engrossed with its scientific and metaphysical approach to life. Her subconscious undoubtedly knew she would follow the direction of the hexagram, for it always speaks to you in a way, in a symbol that you will follow and understand. It will not speak to you in a voice of someone you dislike or disapprove of.

It spoke literally to her, where it revealed the right doctor she should see for the healing of her foot. So the Lord makes—the Lord as the Lordly power within you. There's only one power in you now. He makes himself known in a vision and will speak to man in a dream. That's what your Bible says, because it also says, *"In a dream, in a vision of the night, when deep sleep falleth upon man, slumbering upon the bed, He openeth the ears of men and sealeth their instructions."*

There's only one being, and that power is within you. It's called the life principle, it's called the living spirit Almighty. It's called by many names, but remember, you do not put self-expansion into the seed. You do not give vitality to the seed. It won't grow in your pocket, you put the seed in the ground and you water and fertilize it.

As Judge Troward, author of inimitable textbooks, says, "Your quiet contemplation of your desire as an accomplished fact is the way to pray. The feeling of pleasure and restfulness in foreseeing the certain accomplishment of our desire is the way to get the answer to your prayer. The operation is that of a gardener."

And it is more or less an analog of a gardener. We do not put self-expansion or vitality into the seed. We sow it. Then we water it and fertilize it, knowing that it's going to expand and unfold in a wonderful way if you water it with faith, with expectancy, with understanding. Then wonders will begin to happen in your life.

. . .

A thought is the most powerful force in the universe. Your word is a thought expressed. If you are in a position of authority, your thought or word can direct how missiles, nuclear energy, dynamite, or thermonuclear weapons are to be used. Your thought determines how electricity is to be used.

Likewise, your thought directs the operation of your life. Your subconscious mind could be likened to an iceberg; ninety percent of it is below the surface. It is your subconscious mind that does the work according to the orders given by your conscious mind. What you think with your conscious mind, you produce with your subconscious.

Dr. Arthur Thomas is minister of the Church of Religious Science in Pasadena, but he was the minister in Reno, Nevada for a long time. He had been a captain in the British Navy before that, and more recently, he had been in the wholesale business as well as in real estate in Los Angeles.

About ten years ago he started attending my lectures on Sunday mornings. He said, "I realized suddenly that my thought was the only creative power of which I was aware, and I was going to create what I really wanted." Consequently, he began to affirm to himself frequently, "I am a minister now. I am teaching the truths of life to people." This is what he used to say to himself.

Every night he would imagine he was expatiating on the great truths to a wonderful group of men and women in a church. Not any particular church, just a church. You can do that in your mind, can't you?

He continued to think along these lines for a month or so when he decided to take the ministerial course at the Institute of Religious Science here in Los Angeles. Confident of the end result, as he had already imagined and felt as true the reality of that which he imaged in his mind, he passed all tests and examinations in divine order. He was offered the church immediately after finishing his seminary course.

He is now doing exactly what he decreed mentally. He knew that his subconscious mind would respond mathematically and accurately according to his thinking process. That's the meaning of, *According to your faith is it done unto you.* And of course it is.

During a trip to Mexico two years ago I visited its famous pyramids. There I met a minister who had a pronounced facial tic which was very aggravating and humiliating to him. He had received alcoholic injections which were supposed to deaden or paralyze the nerve, but after some months the tic flared up again.

The condition became very acute when he spoke before his congregation or other social gatherings.

He had reached the point where he was actually contemplating resigning because of the comments of people and his own sense of embarrassment. The tic was in the right eye, and this condition would go on while he was talking. As he said to me, "A lot of people think I'm dating someone or I'm flirting with them," he said.

After a prolonged discussion, I remarked that I had a deep inner feeling that he had a pronounced sense of hurt plus a guilt complex, which he was unwilling to face subjectively and objectively. This tic condition was affecting his right eye, which could possibly symbolize something he didn't want to look at in his home or office. There was some reason why his subconscious mind was selecting his face and his right eye as a scapegoat.

He then admitted freely that he no longer believed in what he was teaching, which gave him a guilt complex. Moreover, he was afraid to resign because he felt he could not make a living outside the ministry. He deeply resented members of his board who criticized whenever he deviated from the orthodox standard of teaching.

All this nervous pressure was converted by his subconscious mind into a tic. The affliction compensated him in a morbid way for his failure to be honest and forthright and admit to his congregation that he no longer believed according to the directives and dogma of the church.

He freely admitted this to me, and I suggested to him in turn that on the following Sunday when he returned from his vacation, he should speak freely from the platform and tell his congregation that he was resigning since he no longer believed what he was preaching. He understood that to teach one thing and to believe another created a powerful negative conflict in the mind, resulting in mental and physical disorder.

That next week he spoke from the depths of his heart to his congregation and then resigned. In a letter to me, he said, "I felt a tremendous relief, and a great sense of peace came over me. My constant affirmation was, 'Thou will show me the path of life,' and one of my former board members gave me a position as personnel director for the organization, where I am happy." He added, "What you said is true. Oftentimes, the explanation is the cure."

If you have a problem, mental, physical, or emotional, ask yourself, "What am I turning away from? What is it I don't want to face? Am I hiding my resentment and hostility toward someone?" Face the problem, and solve it with the knowledge of your deeper mind, knowing that the life principle always seeks to heal, to restore. *"He restoreth my soul."*

The life principle never condemns. It never punishes. It never judges, it can't. All judgment is given to the son, and the son is your own mind. You pass judgment on yourself by your own thought, the verdict in your own mind.

Remember, the life principle cannot punish you, cannot judge you. You judge yourself, and you fashion your own destiny, for as you think in your heart or your subconscious, so are you.

Realize that thoughts are things. What you feel, you attract. What you imagine, you become. Then wonders will begin to happen in your life because there's only one power, and that power is within you.

You're the captain on the bridge. You're giving the orders. Your subconscious mind will take the impression you give it and bring it to pass, whether it's true or not. Therefore, accept only those things which are true.

*   *   *

A few years ago I wrote a book in Honolulu. I had a most interesting conversation with an old friend who I had known previously in India, whom I'll call Harry. Harry is a medical doctor who has tremendous faith in spiritual healing, and is very familiar with the many schools of healing. He practiced clairvoyance and astral excursions for many years. His daughter was studying in Honolulu and had been very ill, actually at the point of death.

A cable was sent to him in Calcutta, and the moment he received it, he adopted a yoga posture, closed his eyes, and got into a passive, quiet, receptive state of mind. He visualized his fourth-dimensional or astral body emerging through his head with all his faculties, and he decreed firmly, knowingly, and with deep conviction, "I want to appear instantly to my daughter and minister to her."

I might interject here that astral traveling, fourth-dimensional traveling, has gone on since the dawn of time. In other words, man can live outside his body. Modern science knows that today. You can see, hear, feel, smell, travel independent of your physical organism, and you can see without eyes and hear without ears. Nature leaves no gaps and makes no mistakes, so it was intended that you use all these faculties, transcendentally of your environment. Notice the wonders of your subconscious mind.

So he said, "I want to appear to my daughter and minister to her," repeated this command about six times and then dropped off into a profound slumber. Immediately he found himself at his daughter's bedside.

She was asleep but awakened immediately and exclaimed to him, "Dad, why didn't you tell me you were coming? Help me." He placed his hands upon her and chanted certain religious phrases, and told her, "You will arise in a few hours and be well."

She had a wonderful healing. Her fever immediately subsided, and she shouted to the nurse, "I'm healed. I'm well. My father was here, and he healed me."

The nurse thought she was raving, but the resident physician confirmed the silent, inner knowing of her soul that she was indeed perfectly well. However both laughed at her story about the visitation of her father from India. The nurse was puzzled and perplexed and said to the daughter, "How could your father or anybody else get in from downstairs through closed doors? I saw no one enter your room."

The daughter explained to the nurse, "Oh, my father visited me in his fourth-dimensional body. He laid his hands on me and prayed with me."

The nurse said, "I don't believe in ghosts, apparitions, or voodoo," and the girl realized that further explanations would be useless.

Harry said that he was perfectly conscious the whole time. Considering the distance between Calcutta and Honolulu and the time difference, he discovered that he'd been absent from his physical body for just ten minutes in all.

He realized his presence gave a tremendous transfusion of faith, confidence, and courage to his daughter, which impregnated her subconscious mind, and according to his belief and that of his daughter, it was done unto her. These are the wonders of the friend within you. That's the deeper mind.

* * *

Your subconscious mind is never short of ideas. There are within an infinite number of ideas, ready to flow into your conscious mind and appear as cash in your pocketbook. This process will continue to go on in your mind regardless of whether the stock market goes up or down, whether the pound sterling or dollar drops in value. Your wealth is never dependent on stocks, bonds, or money in the bank. These are really only symbols. Necessary and useful, but symbols.

As you go to sleep at night, say to yourself, "Wealth, success, wealth, success." When you admit there is such a thing as wealth, you admit there is such a thing as success. The infinite can't fail. The infinite is within you, and you're born to win. You're born to succeed. Just take these two words, wealth and success. What happens? They activate the latent powers of your subconscious, and you're compelled to succeed. You're compelled to be wealthy.

The point I wish to emphasize is that if you convince your subconscious mind that wealth is forever circulating in your life, and there's always a surplus, you will always have wealth, regardless of the form it takes.

Right now it has taken the form as an amalgam of copper and tin or zinc or something. It hasn't any intrinsic value. You know it's a piece of paper, don't you? The only value it has is what we place upon it. The government says this $10 bill will buy so many oranges, and so on. Yet all it is is a piece of paper. It isn't even silver or gold.

There are people who claim they're always trying to make ends meet. They seem to have a great struggle to meet their obligations. Have you listened to their conversation? In many instances, their conversation runs along the same vein, constantly condemning those who have succeeded in life, who have raised their heads above the crowd.

Perhaps they're saying, "That fellow has a racket. He's ruthless. He's a crook." This is why they lack. They're condemning the thing they desire and want. The reason they speak critically of their more prosperous associates is because they're envious and covetous of the other's prosperity.

The quickest way to make wealth take wings and fly away is to be envious and jealous, or criticize and condemn others who have more wealth than you. You can rest assured that will impoverish you and bring more lack into your experience.

There is one emotion which is the main cause of lack of wealth in the lives of many people. Most people learn this the hard way: it's envy. If you see a competitor depositing large sums of money in the bank and you only have a meager amount to deposit, does it make you envious?

The way to overcome this emotion is to say to yourself, "Isn't it wonderful? I rejoice in that man's prosperity. I wish for him greater and greater wealth." You're selfish when you do that because what you're wishing for him, you're creating in your own mind, body, and experience.

To entertain envious or jealous thoughts is devastating, because it places you in a very negative, destructive position. Wealth flows from you instead of to you. If you're ever annoyed or irritated by the prosperity of another, claim immediately that you truly wish for him wealth and success in every possible way. This will neutralize the negative thoughts in your mind and cause an ever-greater measure of wealth to flow to you, by the law of your subconscious mind.

If you are worried and critical about someone whom you claim is making money dishonestly, cease thinking about him. You know such a person is using the law of mind negatively, and the law of mind will take care of him. Your Bible tells you in the 37th Psalm *"Fret not about evildoers. They're the workers of iniquity."* Read the 37th Psalm, it's a great eye-opener.

Be careful not to criticize a man for the reasons we just said. Remember, the obstacle to wealth is in your own mind. You can now destroy that mental block. You may do this by getting on good mental terms with everybody, wishing for everyone what you wish for yourself. As you do, wonders will begin to happen in your life. It is your right to be rich.

You're here to lead the abundant life. You're here to be happy, radiant, and free. You should therefore have all the wealth you need to lead a full, happy, prosperous life. Of course you should. You're here to grow, expand, and unfold spiritually, mentally, materially, and professionally.

You have the inalienable right to fully develop and express yourself along all lines. You should surround yourself with beauty and luxury. Why be satisfied with just enough to go around when you can enjoy the riches of your subconscious mind?

Make friends with money and you will always have a surplus. Your desire to be rich is the desire for a fuller, happier, more wonderful life. It is a cosmic urge. It is not only good, but very good. Money is a symbol. It means not only freedom from want, but beauty, luxury, abundance, and refinement. It's a symbol of the economic health of the nation.

When your blood is circulating freely in your body, you're healthy. When money is circulating freely in your life, you're economically healthy. Engage your friend; your friend is your subconscious. It'll give you all the wealth you need to do what you want to do when you want to do it.

When people begin to hoard money, put it away in tin boxes and become charged with fear, there's economic illness. Money has taken many forms as a medium of exchange through the centuries: salt, beads, and trinkets of various kinds. In the early times, a man's wealth was determined by the number of sheep and oxen he had. Now we use currency and other negotiable instruments, as it is much more convenient to write a check than to carry sheep and cattle around with us to pay our bills.

As you go to sleep at night, every night, practice a very simple technique. Repeat the words, "Wealth, success, wealth, success." You admit there's such a thing as infinite wealth. Walk down the street, go out in the country. Can you count the stars or the sands on the seashore?

You're born to win, to succeed. The infinite can't fail. The infinite is within you, so is wealth and success. Use these words, quietly, easily, and feelingly. Do it over and over again as a lullaby.

You'll be amazed at the result. Wealth will flow to you in avalanches of abundance. This is an example of the magic power of your subconscious.

Programming
Your Subconscious

Suppose a physiologist or psychiatrist hypnotized you. In that state, your conscious, reasoning mind is suspended, and your subconscious is amenable to suggestion. If he suggested that you were the president of the United States, your subconscious would accept the statement as true. Your subconscious does not reason, choose, or differentiate as does your conscious mind. You would assume all the airs of importance and dignity that you believe to be the legitimate concomitant of that position.

If you were given a glass of water and told you were drunk, you would play the role of a drunkard to the best of your ability. If you told the psychiatrist that you were allergic to timothy grass, and he placed a glass of distilled water under your nose telling you at the same time that it was timothy grass, you would generate all the symptoms of an allergic attack, and the physiological and physical reactions would be the same as if the water were actually timothy grass.

If you were told that you were a beggar on Skid Row, your demeanor would immediately change, and you would assume the attitude of humble suppliance with an imaginary tin cup in your hand. In short, you may be made to believe that you're anything, such as a statue, dog, soldier, or swimmer, and you will act the part suggested with amazing fidelity to the nature of the suggestion, insofar as your knowledge of the characteristics of the thing that is suggested.

Another important point to remember is that your subconscious mind always accepts the dominant of two ideas. That is, it accepts your conviction without question, whether your premise is true or absolutely false. The modern scientific, straight-line thinker looks at God as the infinite intelligence within his subconscious mind. He doesn't care whether people call it the superconscious, unconscious, subjective mind, living spirit Almighty, or whether they call the supreme intelligence Allah, Brahma, Jehovah, Reality, Spirit, or the All-Seeing Eye. The point is that it's there within you.

All the powers of the infinite are within you. God is spirit, however, and the spirit has no face, form, or figure. It is timeless, spaceless, and eternal. The same spirit indwells every man. This is why Paul says, "*Thou stir up the gift of God which is in thee.*"

You're also told the Kingdom of God is within you, in the Book of Luke. Yes, God is in your thought, your feeling, your imagination. In other words, the invisible part of you is God. God is the life principle in you, boundless love, absolute harmony, infinite intelligence knowing that you can contact this invisible power through your thoughts, and strip the whole process of prayer from mystery, superstition, doubt, and wonder.

The Bible tells you the word was God. The word is a thought expressed, as you know, and based on what you've already heard, every thought is creative and tends to manifest itself in your life according to the nature of your thought. It stands to reason that any time you discover the creative power you have discovered God, for there's only one creative power not two, three, or a thousand—just one.

Hear O Israel. Israel means illumined awakened man, the Lord, the supreme power. Our God is one Lord, one power, one presence, one cause, and one substance.

•   •   •

Many of us were conditioned negatively when we were young. All of us were susceptible to suggestion when we were young, highly impressionable. For example, supposing a man is a sourpuss, or he has a nasty temper, and he complains about it. He can sit down every night prior to sleep and also in the morning and the afternoon, and he can affirm as follows.

He can write these in his subconscious. He can reprogram his mind. He can redirect it. He can write upon it, and the nature of the subconscious is compulsive, therefore he'll be compelled to become genial, cordial, a man of goodwill. This is what he should say.

> "Henceforth, I shall grow more good-humored. I shall have more joy and happiness and inner peace of mind. Every day I am becoming more and more lovable and understanding. I am now becoming the center of cheer, cordiality, and goodwill to all those around me, infecting them with good humor. This happy, joyous, and cheerful mood is now becoming my normal, natural state of mind, and I am grateful."

He can take these statements, reiterate them, repeat them, and remind himself that he's writing these in his deeper mind. Whatever is impressed in his subconscious mind comes forth as form, as function, as experience, and event, for out of the heart of the subconscious are the issues of life.

Many people have been victims of negative suggestions or negative conditioning or programming when

they were very young. In all ages, the power of suggestion has played a part in the life and thought of man in
every period of time and in each country of the earth.
In many parts of the world it is the controlling power
in religion. Suggestion may be used to discipline and
control ourselves.

There are constructive suggestions, and there are
also negative ones. Suggestion can be used to take
control, command over others who do not know the
laws of mind. In its constructive form it is wonderful
and magnificent. In its negative aspects it is one of the
most destructive of all response patterns of the mind,
resulting in inferiority, patterns of failure, suffering,
sickness, and disease.

From infancy on, the majority of us have been given
many negative suggestions. Negative "programming"
would be a better word. Not knowing how to reject
them or thwart them, we unconsciously accept them.
Here are some of the negative suggestions resulting in
negative programming of your subconscious mind:

You were told, "Oh, you can't do that." Maybe
someone said to you, "You'll never amount to anything." Now you have an inferiority complex. They
said, "You mustn't do that. You'll fail. You don't have
a chance. You're all wrong. It's no use. It's not what
you know but who you know. The world is going to

the dogs. What's the use? Nobody cares. It's no use trying so hard."

Others said to you, "You're too old now. Forget it. Your memory is failing. Things are getting worse and worse. Life is an endless grind." Others said to you, "Love is for the birds, and you just can't win. Pretty soon you'll be bankrupt. Watch out, you'll get the virus. You can't trust a soul."

If you accept these negative suggestions, you'll program your subconscious mind in a very negative way. You'll have a sense of inferiority, inadequacy, and a sense of fear, unless as an adult you program your subconscious mind constructively, which is a reconditioning therapy. The impressions made on you in the past can cause behavior patterns that cause failure in your personal and social life.

Programming is a means of releasing you from the mass of negative verbal conditioning that might otherwise distort your life pattern, making the development of good habits difficult. Pick up the paper any day and you can read dozens of items that could sow the seeds of futility, fear, worry, anxiety, and impending doom. If you accept them, these thoughts of fear could cause you to lose the will for life.

Knowing that you can reject all these negative suggestions by giving your subconscious mind constructive auto-suggestions, you counteract all these destructive ideas. Check regularly on the negative suggestions that people make to you. You don't have to be influenced by destructive negative suggestions. All of us have suffered from it in our childhood and in our teens.

If you look back you can easily recall how parents, friends, relatives, teachers, and associates contributed in a campaign of negative suggestions. Study the things said to you and you will discover much of it was in the form of propaganda. The purpose of much of what was said was to control you or instill fear into you. The negative suggestions go on in every home, office, factory, and club.

You will find that many of these negative suggestions are for the purpose of making you think, feel, and act as others want you to and in ways that are to their advantage. That's negative programming of your deeper mind.

There is a right way to program your subconscious mind. Every morning of your life, you can sit steady, quiet, get relaxed, and affirm as follows:

"Divine law and order governs my life. Divine right action reigns supreme. Divine success is mine. Divine harmony is mine. Divine peace fills my soul. Divine love saturates my whole being. Divine abundance is mine. Divine love goes before me today and every day, making straight, joyous, and glorious my way."

This is the way a marine captain programmed his subconscious mind during World War II. He reiterated these truths frequently. Gradually, by repetition, faith, and expectancy, they entered into his subconscious mind, and whatever is impressed in the subconscious is compulsive. Therefore he was compelled to lead a life of harmony, peace, and love. This is how he programmed his mind every morning and every night:

"The Lord is my pilot. I shall not drift. He lighteth me across the dark waters. He steer at me in the deep channels. He keepeth my log. He guideth me by the star of holiness for His namesake. Yet though I sail through the thunders and tempests of life, I shall dread no danger, for thou art with me. Thy love and thy care, they shelter me. Thou prepares to harbor before me in the homeland of eternity. Thou anointest the waves with oil. My ship rideth calmly. Surely sunlight and starlight shall favor me on the voyage I take, and I will rest in the ports of my God forever."

That's by Jay Rogers, a merchant marine captain, written during World War II. You can do that, too, every morning before you step into your automobile. You can sit down and repeat that, remind yourself of these truths.

What are you doing? Aren't you programming? Aren't you writing into your subconscious mind? Aren't you feeding it life-giving patterns? As you reiterate these things and remind yourself and announce these truths and believe in them, they sink into your subconscious mind and they become compulsive. For the nature of your subconscious mind is compulsive.

Last year, I was speaking in New Orleans at the Unity Temple there, and a woman said, "There was a man used to come here, and he used to say quite frequently, 'There are lot of holdups in my neighborhood. I remain open at night rather late, and I am going to be held up one of these nights. I'll probably be shot, too.' They told him stop making these negative suggestions. Stop thinking along that line."

Well, he kept on doing it. He didn't pay any attention. He kept programming his subconscious negatively, and he was held up, and he was also shot.

That's the wrong way. He could have taken the 91st Psalm and said "*I dwell in the secret place of the most high. I abide in the shadow of the Almighty. I will say of the Lord, He is my refuge, my fortress. My God, in Him will I trust. Surely He shall cover me with His feathers, and under His wing shall I rest, and the truth shall be my shield and buckler. I shalt not be afraid, for the terror by night or the arrow that flieth by day."*

He could have reiterated these truths. He could have realized the love of God surrounded him and enfolded him. Where he was, God was. He could have said to himself, "Thou art my hiding place. Thou will compass me about with songs of deliverance." Then he would build up an immunity to all harm. These are spiritual antibodies that immunize you. You become God intoxicated, and that's the right way to program your mind.

A few years ago, a detective told me about a woman who was raped and strangled. In checking her apartment, he found clippings of rape going back 20 years. *"That which I greatly fear,"* Job says, *"has come upon me."* She was programming her subconscious mind, negatively of course, and she experienced that what she feared. That's the wrong thing to do. Fear is faith upside down. Fear is faith in the wrong thing.

We've had politicians running for office who've said to newsmen, "I've lived in constant fear of assassination." Even though he had bulletproof glass in front of him when he spoke, he announced that to the reporters.

Of course he didn't know the laws of mind, perhaps didn't know that he could cast out fear, but he could. *"I will fear no evil for thou art with me. Thy rod and thy staff, they comfort me."* The rod means the power, and the staff is your authority to call upon. It will answer you.

"One with God is a majority, and if God be for me, who can be against me? Thou art my hiding place. Thou shall compass me about with songs of deliverance." The politician could have said, *"I dwell in a secret place. I'm surrounded by the sacred circle of God's eternal love. The whole armor of God surround me. Wherever I go, the light of God surrounds me, enfolds me, and enwraps me."*

He would render himself invulnerable, invincible, and impervious to all harm. That's the right way to program your subconscious mind. You can build up that immunity. *"As a man thinketh in his heart or subconscious, so is he, so does he act, so does he experience, so does he express."* This is the law. I'm not talking about thinking in the head. I'm talking about thinking in your heart, your own subconscious. Whatever is impressed there is expressed.

* * *

Remember that when you're dealing with your subconscious, you're dealing with the power of the Almighty. It's the power that moves the world. It's the power that moves the galaxies in space. It's Almighty. There's nothing to oppose it.

Consciousness is God. Unconditioned consciousness sometimes is called awareness. *"I am living spirit Almighty."* Your consciousness is the union of your conscious and subconscious mind. It's the sum total of your acceptances, your beliefs, your opinions, and your convictions. That's God, the only God you'll ever know. Your thought and feeling create your destiny. Consciousness is God because it is the only creative power in your life, and your thought and feeling is the father of all experience.

If you talk about the father within, what father is everything? Your own thought and feeling, your conscious and subconscious. Whatever your conscious and subconscious mind agree on, meaning the brain and the heart, comes to pass. True or false, good or bad.

You're the one who's choosing. You mold and fashion your own destiny. Your faith in God is your fortune, and your faith should be in the goodness of God in the land of the living, in the guidance of God, in the harmony of God, in the beauty and glory of the infinite. That's where it should be.

You're told, *"No manifestation come within needs that I, the father, draweth."* The father is your own thought and feeling. So, whatever experiences come to us, there is an equivalent pattern in our subconscious mind. There's always a cause, and that cause is in our mind.

A man said to me that he wanted to succeed and advance in life. In reality, he didn't. He had a sub-conscious pattern of failure. He had a sense of guilt and felt he should be punished. With his conscious mind he worked very hard, and he said to himself in his intellect, "Oh, I work very hard." But in his deeper mind he was programmed and conditioned to failure.

He had a sense of unworthiness and a belief which compelled him to fail. He had a picture of failing in his mind. He felt he should be punished, that he was a sinner. The law of your subconscious is compulsive. That's the Almighty power. It's the power of God.

He learned to reprogram his mind by realizing that he was born to win, born to succeed, born to triumph, for the infinite power is within him. It knows no fail-ure. It's Almighty. It created all things. There's noth-ing to oppose it, challenge it, thwart it, or vitiate it, for it is Almighty. It's the only power.

Furthermore, he learned he was punishing him-self. He started every morning and night and also during the day, and this is what he affirmed. Now, he was writing this down with his conscious mind, and this is what he wrote:

> "I am born to win. I'm born to succeed in my prayer life, in my relationship with people, in my chosen work, and in all phases of my life, for the

infinite is within me, and the infinite can't fail. It's the power of the Almighty moving through me. It's my strength. It's my power. It's my wisdom."

Then he said,

"Success is mine. Harmony is mine. Beauty is mine. Divine love is mine. Abundance is mine."

He repeated these truths. He reflected upon them. He reminded himself, driving along the road, before he went in to see a customer. He announced these truths regularly and systematically, and he didn't deny what he affirmed.

Gradually he became a tremendous success, because he succeeded in impregnating his subconscious mind by repetition, reminding himself, announcing these things, teaching his thoughts to dwell upon the great affirmatives of life.

*　*　*

As you do this regularly and systematically, wonders will happen in your life. When you were born no one had to tell you how to find the mother's breast. There was a subjective wisdom guiding you, directing you. Yes, the Bible says, *"I will write my laws in your inward parts. I will write them in your heart. I will be your God, and you shall be my people."*

All the powers of God are within you, and the laws and the truths of God are written in your own subjective mind. All the vital organs were controlled when you were born, when you were sound asleep. Every night of your life that same intelligence governs all the vital organs of your body, your breathing, your inspiration, circulation of your blood, your digestion, your heartbeat, and so on. That's the God presence within you.

The presence and power of God are within you. The great eternal truths are there. They were inscribed in your heart before you were born, but all of us have been programmed since birth. Millions of people have been programmed with certain fears, false beliefs, taboos, strictures, and superstitions.

As Quimby said in 1847, "Every child is like a little white tablet." Then everybody comes along and scribbles something on it, grandmother, grandfather, clergyman, father, mother, sisters, brothers. We receive an avalanche of sights and sounds, beliefs and opinions, don'ts, fears, and doubts.

You weren't born with any fears at all. You weren't born with any prejudices. You weren't born with any creeds or beliefs or any false or weird concepts of God or life. Where did you get them? Someone gave them to you. Someone programmed you, perhaps negatively.

Many were told they were sinners in the hands of an angry God. I have talked to women. Beautiful, attractive, and well educated women. They wear black stockings. They think it's a sin to use rouge or makeup of any kind or wear gold. "Oh, that's a terrible sin." All these are sins when you look at them. They're frustrated, bottled up, inhibited, unhappy.

I tell them to wake up, to dress for God. There's nothing in the universe evil. The whole world was here when they were born. All the birds sing for you, and all the animals in the world are here, all the stars are in the sky for you to adore and to worship and to be delighted with.

So I tell them, "You're here to dance, and so go ahead and learn to dance, for the universe is the dance of God." I tell them, "Take lessons in golf, play music, do all the things you're not doing. Attend college, take lectures in public speaking, meet men, go out and take courses in Spanish or many other things. You're here to lead a full and happy life. You're here to live in an objective world, have recreation, have fun, merriment, and joy and creativity, and express yourself. Of course you're here to meditate and pray, too."

We're living in a subjective and objective world. There's nothing evil in the universe. God pronounced everything good, therefore, there's nothing evil in dancing or playing cards or anything of that nature.

There's nothing evil in looking at a movie, a constructive one, nothing evil in any of those things. Nothing good or bad, but thinking makes it so.

Then I explained to them, "You're frustrated, you're sick, you're unhappy," and I taught them how to attract a man into their life. I said, "You should be married. You should have love. Every woman wants to be loved and cosseted, appreciated." She likes to receive attention. She wants to feel needed and wanted, and if she says she doesn't, she's sick. Every woman does.

Then they learn a simple law. They go out and do all these things. "Do the thing you're afraid to do and the death of fear is certain." I tell them, "You've been brainwashed. You've been programmed negatively and destructively, and the will of God for you is a greater measure of joy, of happiness, of love, of peace of mind."

They learn the law of attraction. You should see some of them now coming to the Wilshire Ebell Theatre, beautifully dressed, and they have some makeup on too, and they have beautiful rings, sometimes a marriage ring. They have transformed. They have reprogrammed their mind.

"Infinite spirit attracts to me the ideal man who harmonizes with me in every way, shape, and form. He is spiritual-minded. He loves my ideals; I love his ideals. He doesn't want to make me over, and I don't want to make him over. He comes without encumbrances. He's the man sent from God. There are harmony, peace, love, and understanding between us."

That's the prayer I give them, and then I say, "Write that down in your subconscious. Do it with interest. Gradually, like a seed, it will lie in your deeper mind and come to pass in ways you know not of."

· · ·

I was taught when I was young that if a boy were indoctrinated with a certain religious belief until he was seven that no one could change him. Of course they can be changed, but it's rather difficult. The boy is being brainwashed, but they were referring to that negative conditioning of the mind.

When we're young we're susceptible, we're impressionable, and teachable. We are amenable to suggestion. We don't have the sense to reject the negative suggestions, and we accept the many false beliefs and erroneous concepts in regards to God, life, and the universe.

Where did you get your creed or your religious belief? You certainly weren't born with it. Is it true? Is it reasonable? Is it illogical, unreasonable? Is it unscientific? If it's unscientific, illogical, and unreasonable, it can't be true.

There is Pat, for example. He believes the cards are stacked against him. Some fortune teller told him that, I suppose. The cards are not stacked against him. The universe is for him, but he is enthroned in that concept and he believes it. His subconscious mind accepts it. This false belief creates a quarrel in his mind, and he thinks people are working against him, that misfortune would follow him, that some sort of a jinx is after him. He made that law for himself, and it controls him and governs him.

Man's subconscious assumptions, beliefs, and convictions dictate, control, and manipulate all of his conscious actions. The late Dr. David Seabury had told me about a man who was partially crippled. He had little or no education, and as an experiment in suggestion Dr. Seabury pretended to analyze his potentialities based upon the idea that his mental faculties and character traits were indicated by the configuration of his head, as well as the lines in his hand.

Seabury told this man, "You are destined to become a great evangelist, a great preacher. God intended you to go forth and preach in a wonderful, wonderful way."

This man became active in his particular church, and he became an outstanding preacher. He accepted and believed that God had ordained him to become a great preacher, and according to his belief, it was done unto him. It was as simple as that.

There is only one power, one presence. Your thought and feeling fathers all your experience. How are you programmed in your subconscious mind? The creative power is one.

You know one of the greatest of all truths? *"Here, O, Israel, the Lord thy God is one Lord."* Israel means a prince ruling with God. Israel means any man who knows his I Am-ness to be the Lord, God Almighty, to be sovereign and supreme, and he gives all his allegiance, devotion, and loyalty to that one power, the living spirit within him. He gives no power to any created thing, to any man, woman, or child in this universe.

Your Lord, our master, is your dominant idea or belief, your conviction. That's your Lord. Suppose you believe in a God of love. Supposing that belief is enthroned in your mind, and you really believe it. That that's the only presence and power, it's dominance supreme, and you give it all your allegiance, loyalty, and devotion. Then that is your Lord; it's your master. Then you'll lead a charmed life.

In England, some men believe that every November they're going to get rheumatism. They attribute it to the climate and change of atmosphere and of course they do receive it. They have programmed their mind. They expect it, and according to their belief or expectancy, it is done unto them.

Say you have one man in the house who gets his rheumatism regularly in November. But his brother, living in the same house, eating the same food, born of the same parents, working the same farm, doesn't get rheumatism at all. He believes in health and long life.

Other people believe the night air will give them a cold, or they'll get the sniffles if someone sneezes in the office, and according to their belief is it done unto them. Others in the office do not get the cold or the flu at all. Some people, when their feet get wet, they say, "Oh, I'm going to get my death of cold. I'm going to get a chill now." The water is only H_2O. The water never said, "I'll give you a cold or the sniffles." It's all belief or negative conditioning. The night air is innocuous. It's hydrogen and nitrogen, oxygen, and some other gases. It's harmless. It is their belief that is the cause of it.

Your belief is your Lord and your Master. There be Lords many, but there's one Lord, the Father of all of whom are all things. When a person sneezes in the office, it doesn't mean you're going to catch a cold, or there's some germ there that's going to attack you. Others in the office don't get the cold at all, but if you believe that, then you'll bring it on yourself. You may attribute it to germs in the office or the air. Others are immune to it.

There are some people who sit under a fan all day long. They don't suffer from a draft or get a stiff neck. If you believe you're going to get a stiff neck, you will. But the fan is simply molecules moving in space at velocity. That's all.

You built a law about sneezing, or about a fan, or about the air or the water. Then you point to the fan or to the night air and say that you are now ill because of them. You point to these things and you say where your belief is corroborated, but others deny that and laugh at it.

You've made a law for yourself because if it were a law, then anyone sitting under a fan would get a stiff neck. Everyone in the world sitting under a fan would be subject to that law, but it's not a law at all. It's a law you make for yourself. The fan is absolutely innocuous, absolutely harmless.

Stop making laws for yourself. It's like the person who makes a law that he's allergic to a red rose. But in talking to him, you'll find that the girl that he was going with some years ago used to wear a red rose all the time, and she ran off with another man. He has never released her, forgiven her, and there's resentment lurking in his subconscious mind.

So when he sees another girl with a red rose, he sneezes. It's not the girl, it's not the rose. It's the poisoned pocket in his own subconscious. He should have rejoiced and said, "I wish for that girl health and happiness and peace and rejoice that she's found the man of her dreams, and God be with her." Then he would be doing the right thing, and he would be very selfish when he did that because he'd be blessing himself. For what you wish for in others, you're wishing for yourself.

·   ·   ·

Externals have no power except through your own consciousness. Your consciousness is the union of your conscious and subconscious mind. Your conscious mind chooses.

The alcoholic has repeatedly suggested to himself weakness, inadequacy, inferiority, and rejection. After a while, as he continues to make these negative suggestions and continues to drink to bolster his courage, he's denying the divinity within him, the power of the Almighty within him. And after a while, through repeated negative suggestions, he has lost the choice.

Now he takes one drink and he's off to the races. He's a compulsive drinker, he is an inebriate. Before then he had choice. He could say, "I'll take one or two drinks, and that's all." Now, he hasn't. He's lost that power, for the subconscious is the only power in the world that can say, "I will," and mean it.

He's been rejecting the only presence and power, and he's implanted these negative suggestions by repetition into his deeper mind. He's referred to sometimes as a compulsive drinker, or there's also the compulsive gambler and the compulsive eater, and so forth, all based upon negative suggestions repeated over and over again into the deeper mind.

He says, "I will not drink." He may take an oath on the Bible that he'll never take another drink, but all that is nonsense. It's just a joke and farce. He is thinking about and picturing himself at the bar. Actually, he's writing or engraving the idea of drinking deeper into his subconscious mind, and he's compelled to go out and get drunk.

The subconscious mind reacts according to our habitual thinking and imagery. As we sow, we reap. What we impress in our subconscious is expressed. When we feed the computer in the laboratory with false data, then of course, it gives us the wrong answer. We should feed our subconscious mind with life-giving patterns.

The alcoholic can do that. He can say it to his deeper mind, though he must want to give it up and come to a decision, a clear-cut decision. When he desires to give it up, when his desire to give it up is greater than his desire to continue it, he's seventy-five percent healed. Then, the power of the Almighty will back him up and move on his behalf.

So he comes to a decision, claiming, "Sobriety and peace of mind are mine now, from now on. I decree this. I mean it. I'm absolutely sincere. It's irrevocable."

Then he pictures himself doing what he loves to do. If he's an attorney, for example, who's hit bottom and become a panhandler due to alcohol, he's back at court pleading a case for a client. He's behind a polished mahogany desk, talking to his client. He's clean-shaven, he's well dressed, he's talking to the judge, and he's back with his family. He makes there, here; in the future, now.

He is embraced by his daughter and his wife and so forth. He's living the role, and when the desire comes to him to have a drink, he flashes the movie in his mind back with his daughter, his wife, back at home, or back in the office pleading the case.

He is now living that role, and the power of the Almighty backs him up. As he continues to think of freedom, peace of mind, and sobriety, he begins to feel the joy and the wonders of it all, and pictures himself home doing the things he loves to do, and it passes from thought, mood, and picture to function and fact.

Like a seed, it lies in the deeper mind and comes forth as a fruit of the answered prayer. So, he can overcome it, reprogram his subconscious mind to harmony, health, sobriety, and peace of mind, and the power of the Almighty will back him up and take away that craving. He's free, and he forgives himself, of course, for harboring negative thoughts. He forgives everybody else too, by pouring out love, peace, and goodwill on all those around him.

You always know when you've forgiven because you can meet the person in your mind and there's no sting there anymore. Why? Because you poured out love and goodwill and harmony and wished for that person all the blessings of life.

All of us are here to grow, to learn, to release the imprisoned splendor that is within. We're not born fully armed with all our failures. You're here to learn. You're here to sharpen your mental and spiritual tools and take joy in overcoming, in mastering. We're in a world of opposites, and we're told choose ye this day, and we will serve.

You're not an animal. You're not an automaton. You have freedom to choose. You have volition. You have initiative. That's the way you discover your divinity. There is no other way under the sun.

You're not compelled to be good. You're not governed by instinct only. No, you have the opportunity of becoming a holy man or anything you want to. "*I hold before you an open door which no man can shut.*"

Think on whatsoever things are true, lovely, noble, and God-like. You think on these things all day long.

You can begin to recondition your mind. You can picture yourself doing what you long to do because you go where your vision is, and your vision is what you're looking at, what you're thinking about, what you're focused on. And as you continue to focus your attention, that which is lovely and of good report, your deeper mind will respond, and you'll be compelled to move forward in the light, for this Almighty power will move on your behalf.

You can reiterate some great truths as you drive along the road. You say, "There's only one power, one presence, one cause. It's boundless love, it's infinite intelligence, absolute harmony. It's moving in me, through me, and all around me." You can do this as you drive along the road, at lunch, walking the streets, or sitting down to dinner. You can do all these wonderful things. You can reiterate and remind yourself of these great truths.

Choose the good, choose the right action. "Yes, I radiate love, peace, and goodwill to everybody." Keep on reiterating these truths morning, noon, and night. Finally, these truths will sink into your subconscious, for, *"Out of the heart are the issues of life."* Out of the subconscious will come forth whatever you've impressed upon it. Keep thy heart with all diligence.

See to it that nothing but Godlike thoughts and ideas enter into your deeper mind.

Hear the age-old truth again and again until it forms a conviction in your subconscious mind. Hear the absolute truth. *"I am, and there is none else."* One power, one presence, one cause, and one substance. When inscribed in your heart, it becomes compulsive, and you will be compelled to good and to right action.

Some are automatically guided. They have the touch of Midas. They've repeated to themselves over and over again, "Infinite intelligence guides me. Whatever I do will be right. Right action is mine." Morning, noon, and night, they reiterate these truths because there is a principal right action. There is a principle of guidance, and they're activating it from a universal or infinite standpoint.

*   *   *

Grace is the automatic response of your subconscious to your conscious mind, thinking, envisioning. *"I will fear no evil for thou art with me. Thy rod and thy staff, they comfort me. The Lord is my light and my salvation. Whom shall I fear? The Lord is the strength of my life. Of whom shall I be afraid?"* Wonderful truths, and it's marvelous to reiterate that as you drive along the road.

A rabbi on a plane some years ago told me that when he was a young boy, all the boys and girls were taught to read and study Deuteronomy, the sixth chapter—a very beautiful chapter, by the way. They had to realize that God was one and all-powerful. They committed many of these verses to memory.

This is what they had to remember:

"*Hear, O Israel, the Lord our God is one Lord, and thou shall love the Lord, thy God, with all thine heart and with all thine soul and with all thine might. These words which I command thee this day shall be in thine heart.*" Remember, in thine heart.

"*Thou shall teach them diligently unto thine children and shall talk of them when thou sittest in thy house and when thou walkest by the way and when thou liest down, and thou risest up. Thou shall bind them for a sign upon thine hand, and they shall be as frontlets between thine eyes. Thou shall write them upon the posts of thy house and on thy gates. Thou shall fear*"—fear means respect—"*thou shall fear the Lord thy God and serve Him and shall swear by His name. Ye shall not go after other gods or the gods of the people that are around about you because the Lord thy God is a jealous God. Lest the anger of the Lord thy God be kindled against thee and destroy thee,*" for his jealousy in the Bible means you mustn't know another power.

You must not give allegiance to any created thing. You must only recognize the one power only. "*Hear, O Israel, the Lord thy God is one Lord.*"

The idea behind all this is that a firm conviction was to be placed in their heart, because they kept repeating it. *"Thou shall love the Lord thy God."* Love is allegiance and loyalty.

"Thou shall know no other God," meaning that they give power to the one presence and power, and you refuse to give power to anything in the phenomenalistic world, or to any man, woman, or child or sun or moon or star or any created thing. The moment you do, you have no God, *"For I, the Lord,"* as it tells you, *"am jealous."* Jealous in the sense that you don't know another. You are married to the one, allegiance to the one.

Now, this rabbi explained to me that the *mezuzah* is a small case or tube typically of metal or wood, and with an aperture in front that is traditionally attached by Jews to the doorpost of the home. Oftentimes I lived in the same house as a Jewish doctor friend of mine, and he would always touch this as he opened the door.

It contained a piece of parchment inscribed on one side with the verses four to nine of Deuteronomy, which I just quoted. Also, the 13th and 21st verses, such as, *"Thou shall say unto thy son, 'We were Pharaoh's bondsmen in Egypt, and the Lord brought us out of Egypt with a mighty hand.'"* All beautiful verses.

On the other side is the word *Shaddai*, meaning a name for God, the beautiful one, the God of light. It's folded in the case or tube, so that "Shaddai" is visible through the aperture, over the doorpost.

The *phylactery*, in Greek, or *tefillin* in Hebrew, is either of two small black leather cubes with leather straps, containing a piece of parchment inscribed with these verses, the fourth to ninth and 11th and 13th of 21 of the sixth chapter Deuteronomy. They're very beautiful, you ought to read them.

One cube is strapped to the left arm and the other to the forehead during religious services. As you move your arm it reminds you, and if you move your eyes it reminds you, too.

People in all walks of life, down through the ages, wear such things. In India, you get on a plane sometimes and a man comes on with a little Buddha attached to him. Another comes on with an amulet or charm, or they wear Saint Christopher medals or rosary beads. All these things have no power, of course. The little strap, the phylactery or the tefillin, or the mezuzah have no power, but it's simply to remind them that they might begin to contemplate the presence of God in their own hearts and the only presence and power.

Likewise the Christopher medal. This present pope said he never lived, but people do wear the medal and think it's going to protect them. Of course it's only a piece of tin. It has no power, but it's not to be ridiculed because it does remind people of a higher power, and they may believe in it.

It's a reminder of the truths, but the main thing is to incorporate these truths in the soul so you don't need a talisman or an amulet or a charm or a Buddha or a statue. You don't need a mezuzah or a phylactery or any of these things, because you're in communion with God with your thought and you can communicate with Him instantaneously and realize that the Lord is your shepherd, and you shall never want. You can remind yourself, but my God shall supply all you need according to his riches and glory.

"In quietness and in confidence shall be your strength." Remember the truths have to be incorporated in your heart, not in your head, for as a man thinketh in his heart, so is he, and so does he express. You must eat the apple before it becomes your bloodstream.

Likewise, you have to absorb and digest these truths, and it's not vain repetitions but what you absorb and digest and incorporate into your soul. Therefore these truths as you repeat them and begin to dwell upon them, reiterate them, and remind yourself, and go within yourself, or announce these truths to your mind regularly and gradually—again and again and again and again—you'll begin to believe and become convinced that there's only one power.

It'll become a philosophical absolute in your mind that the I Am within you is the only God there is. It's all powerful, all wise. It's the lost word. It's lost to millions. It's there morning, noon, and night. The word is nigh in the mouth and thy heart to will and to do.

Moses tells you that there's no use going over the sea for it, or going up into the air for it. Thy word is nigh in the mouth and thy heart to will and to do. Here are some great truths:

"But my God shall supply all you need according to His riches and glory."

"In quietness and in confidence shall be your strength."

"God who giveth us richly all things to enjoy."

"With God all things are possible."

"Before they call I will answer; while they are yet speaking, I will hear."

"According to your faith, be it unto thee."

"If thou can believe, all things are possible to him that believeth."

"He shall call upon me, and I will answer him. I will be with him in trouble. I will deliver him and honor him. With long life will I satisfy him and show him my salvation."

"All things be ready if the mind be so."

"The Lord is my light and my salvation. Whom shall I fear? The lord is the strength of my life. Of whom shall I be afraid?"

"I will lift up mine eyes unto the hills from whence cometh my help."

"Ask and it shall be given to you. Seek and ye shall find. Knock, and it shall be open unto you."

Here you are told you shall receive that for which you ask. It shall be open to you when you knock. You shall find that for which you are searching. This teaching implies a definiteness of mental and spiritual laws.

There is always a direct response from the infinite intelligence of your subconscious mind to your conscious thinking. Therefore, you can program your subconscious mind constructively, harmoniously, and peacefully. If you ask for bread, you will not receive a stone. You must ask believing if you are to receive.

Your mind moves from the thought to the thing unless there is first an image in the mind it cannot move, for there would be nothing for it to move. When you come to the Ebell on Sunday, first there's an image in your mind. Of course there is. When you think of your mother, you see your mother in your mind.

Your prayer, which is your mental act, must be accepted as an image in your mind before the power in your subconscious will play upon it and make it productive. You must reach a point of acceptance in your mind, an unqualified and undisputed state of agreement. This contemplation should be accompanied by a feeling of joy and restfulness in foreseeing the certain accomplishment of your desire.

The sound basis for the arts and science of true programming of your subconscious is your knowledge and complete confidence that the movement of your conscious mind will gain a definite response from your subconscious mind, which is one with boundless wisdom and infinite power.

The easiest and most obvious way to formulate an idea is to visualize it, to see it in your mind's eye as vividly as if it were alive. You can see with the naked eye only what already exists in the external world. In a similar way, that which you can visualize in your mind's eye already exists in the invisible realms of your mind. Any picture which you have in your mind is the substance of things hoped for and the evidence of things not seen.

What you form in your imagination is as real as any part of your body. The idea and the thought are real and will one day appear in your objective world if you're faithful to your mental image.

The process of thinking forms impressions in your mind. These impressions in turn become manifested as facts and experiences in your life. The builder visualizes the type of building he wants. He sees it as he desires it to be completed. His imagery and thought processes become a plastic mold from which the building will emerge, a beautiful or an ugly one, a skyscraper or a very low one.

His mental imagery is projected as it is drawn on paper. Eventually the contractor and his workers gather the essential materials, and the building progresses until it stands finished, conforming perfectly to the mental patterns of the architect.

. . .

You can use visualization techniques, quiet the wheels of your mind, then picture the loved one whole and perfect. That loved one is telling you, "the miracle of God has happened. I've never felt better in my life."

You see the light in the eye. You see your loved one smile. You don't see them in the hospital, but you see them home doing the things they love to do, radiant and happy and free. You build that up in your mind. That would be called prayer.

Realize a picture is worth a thousand words. William James, the father of American psychology, stressed the fact that the subconscious mind will bring to pass any picture held in the mind and backed by faith. *"Act as though I am, and I will be. Act as though you now are what you long to be.*" Live the role in your mind. Do it again and again and again. Gradually it'll sink into your deeper mind, and one day it will happen as you pray that way.

Let us realize now that we are going to go by the King's highway. We will not turn to the right hand, nor to the left, and your way is God's way, and all God's ways are pleasantness, and all his paths are peace.

Place yourself under God's guidance. Realize God is guiding you now. There's right action in your life, and the Holy Spirit goes before you, making straight, joyous, and glorious your way. Your highway from now on is the royal road of the ancients. It's the middle path of Buddha. It's the straight and narrow gate of Jesus. Your highway is the King's highway, for you're king over all your thoughts, feelings, and emotions.

Send the messengers of love. They're called God's messengers. What are they? God's love, peace, light, and beauty going before you today and every day to make straight, beautiful, joyous, and happy your way.

Always travel the King's highway, and then you will meet God's messengers of peace and joy wherever you go. Go by the mountaintop road knowing that with your eyes stayed on God, there is no evil on your pathway.

Whilst driving a car, riding on a train, bus, airplane, or on foot, realize God's spell is always around you. It is the invisible harbor of God, and you go from point to point freely, joyously, and lovingly. The spirit of the Lord is upon you, making all roads a highway for your God. *"The Lord he is that doth go before thee wheresoever thou goeth."*

Your conviction of God's presence is strong and mighty. Know the spiritual atmosphere in which you dwell goes before you, making straight, beautiful, joyous, happy, and prosperous the way. Realize divine love fills your soul, divine peace floods your mind, and realize God in the midst of you is guiding you now, and the light of God illumines your pathway.

Know there's a perfect law of supply and demand, and you're instantly in touch with everything you need. You're divinely guided in all your ways. You're giving of your talents in a wonderful way. It is written, *"I will bring the blind by a way that they knew not. I will lead them in paths they hath not known."*

God bless you and keep you. The Lord causes faith to shine upon you. The Lord lifts up His countenance upon you, His graces unto you, and gives you peace. *"My peace I leave you, my peace I give you, not as the world giveth, give I unto you. Let not your hearts be troubled. Be not afraid. Trust in God, and do good. Thus shall you walk in the land, and there you will be fed."*

Fed with what? With wisdom, truth, and beauty, with harmony, health, and peace. This is what they said, *"Lord, evermore, give me this bread."*

All the World
Believes A Lie

"All the world believes a lie, so when I am telling the truth, it thinks I am telling a lie."

Who said that? The greatest healer America has ever known, Phineas Parkhurst Quimby, in 1847. He was a marvelous healer and that is one of his favorite statements.

What is that lie? Well the great lie, of course, is that external things are causative. The scientific thinker, the man who thinks, who has any sense at all, will not give power to the phenomenalistic world. The phenomenalistic world is an effect; it's not a cause. The scientific thinker gives power to the creator, not to the created thing.

The infinite presence and power is within you. *"I am the Lord that healeth thee."* So, the miraculous healing power is within you. It's one power. "Hear, O Israel, the Lord thy God is one." One power—not two or three or a thousand, just one. Mathematically, scientifically, spiritually, there can be only one power.

If there were two powers, one would cancel out the other. There would be chaos everywhere. There would be no order, symmetry, or proportion of the universe. There would be a clash of wills, so that would be absurd. There's only one power, so externals are not causative.

There are people who think that the night air gives them a cold or pneumonia. The night air is oxygen and nitrogen, helium and some other gases. It's innocuous, it's harmless. The night air never said, "I'll give you a chill or a cold or the sniffles or pneumonia."

There are people who believe if their feet get wet, as I was taught when I was a boy, "Oh you'll get a cold now," or "You'll get a very bad cold." You may get pneumonia, because your feet were wet. The water is made of H_2O, it's hydrogen and oxygen. It's harmless. The water can't give you a cold or pneumonia or a chill or the sniffles.

Some others say if someone sneezes, "Oh I'm going to catch a cold." Well, to sneeze is simply God's alarm system within you to bring it all to balance. It brings a balance in your body. If you're in a warm room and you go out into the cold atmosphere, you may sneeze. Nature seeks a balance, just like you are born with two fears: the fear of falling and the fear of noise. That's God's alarm system in you.

You're walking down the road, and a car is coming along. It toots a horn, you step aside. You're free from your fear. So the law is, "As a man thinketh in his heart, so is he." The way you think and feel, so are you. Your thought and feeling creates your destiny. Your heart is your subconscious mind, and whatever you impress upon that subconscious mind comes forth as form, function, experience, and event.

You're not subject to forces outside yourself. These are created things. You don't give power to men, women, and children; to the sun, the moon, and the stars. God created all these things. Stars are molecules moving in space. They're molecular, just like your body, as waves of light. The planets are harmless, therefore you don't give power to external things.

You're told there's nothing good or bad, but thinking makes it so. That's an absolute truth. Some people say, "Strawberries give me hives." If that were true, everybody in the world who ate strawberries would get hives, but they don't. That person has made a law for himself. He has a bad relationship with strawberries.

When he says, "Strawberries give me hives," that's a command to his subconscious mind. Of course when he eats strawberries, the subconscious sees the strawberries coming down and says, "The boss wants hives," so it proceeds to give you hives.

These are laws you make for yourself. Or you might say, "I can't eat mushrooms. I get acute indigestion." That's a law you made for yourself. Millions of people eat mushrooms, and they don't get indigestion.

You see, if it were a law, everybody in the world would suffer accordingly. So, don't judge according to appearances. The five senses report an avalanche of sights and sounds and sundry concepts good and bad, but you're not a victim of the five senses. You can reject what you see, what you hear. You can see peace where there is discord, love where there is hatred, joy where there is sadness, light where there is darkness, life where there is so-called death.

You can discipline your senses, and you can taste the sweet savor of God. Taste the truth like you taste an apple. Judge not according to appearances. You're here to separate the sheep from the goats, the false from the real.

Some people say that ragweed gives them asthma or hay fever. If that were true, if that were a cosmic law, everybody in the world who touched ragweed would cry, eyes would begin to tear. They'd get inflammation in their mucosa or paroxysmal attacks.

It's the same thing as when a person says they're sensitive to red roses, or allergic to red roses. If you hypnotized that person and put a glass of distilled water under his nose and said, "This is a red rose," he'd get all the symptoms right there in front of you, but it's still distilled water.

Now tell me honestly, where is the allergy? Isn't it in his mind, a belief? Surely it isn't in the distilled water. He's probably allergic to his wife or to his boss or someone on the next bench. Don't you know that the ragweed and the pollen and all these things are the same substance that's in your own bloodstream?

There's only one substance. God. God is the only presence, power, cause, and substance. Everything is spirit made manifest. So the ragweed or whatever you call it, the pollen or the dust, all these are of God. Everything is spirit made manifest, for there is a spirit and matter. Matter is the lowest degree of spirit, and spirit is the highest degree of matter. They're inter-convertible, interchangeable. They're the same thing.

I visited Dr. Viktor Frankl in Vienna some years ago. He wrote *Man's Search for Meaning*. He practiced what is called logotherapy.* He's a medical doctor, and a distinguished psychiatrist. He had been imprisoned with other doctors in Auschwitz.

---

* Developed by Viktor Frankl, the theory is founded on the belief that human nature is motivated by the search for a life purpose; logotherapy is the pursuit of that meaning for one's life. Frankl's theories were heavily influenced by his personal experiences of suffering and loss in Nazi concentration camps.

He said, "We were anxious to know what would happen, what would be the consequence." For example, they had to stand out in the open air. They took a shower. They had no clothes on. They weren't given a towel or anything at all. It was late autumn. The weather was very cold, and they stood stark naked and still wet from the showers. "In the next few days, our curiosity evolved into surprise," he told me. "We were surprised that we didn't catch cold."

There were many similar surprises in store for the new arrivals. "The medical men among us learned first that the textbooks tell lies," he said. They were angry because the textbooks told lies. They didn't get a cold. They didn't get pneumonia.

Somewhere it is said that man cannot exist without sleep for more than a certain stated number of hours. That's quite wrong.

"I'd been convinced there were certain things I just could not do, that I couldn't sleep without this, or I could not live without that, or the other. We slept in beds which were constructed in tiers. On each tier, measuring about six-and-a-half to eight feet, slept nine men directly on the boards. Two blankets were shared by each nine men. We could, of course, lie only on our sides, crowded and huddled against each other, which had some advantages because of the bitter cold. Though it was forbidden to take shoes up to the bunks, some people did use them secretly as pillows in spite of the fact they were caked with mud.

"Now, I would like to mention a few similar surprises, how much we could endure. We were unable to clean our teeth, yet in spite of that and a severe vitamin deficiency, we had healthier gums than ever before. We had to wear the same shirts for half a year until they had lost all appearance of being shirts. For days, we were unable to wash, even partially, because of frozen water pipes, and yet the sores and abrasions on our hands which were dirty from work in the soil did not separate, that is, unless there was frostbite.

"If someone had asked of us the truth of the statement that flatly defines man as a being who can get used to anything, we would reply, yes, a man can get used to anything, but do not ask us how. Our psychological investigations have not taken us that far yet. Neither had we prisoners reached that point.

"Don't ask us how, because the ways of the infinite are past finding out."

They were all doctors, and according to the textbook they should all get pneumonia, but they didn't.

Nobody died. They were in a higher state of mind, dwelling in a higher level of consciousness.

Dr. Fleet of London told me that during the war she was on a starch diet. She couldn't get the things she was accustomed to. Other people were on starch diets. She said neurotics and psychotics, they performed marvelous things during the war. Under the pressure of the war, they became calm. They administered to people and to all of them, and she said, "We had no vitamins, and our diet was contrary to all science, all scientific findings, and we were healthier than ever before."

This was the same thing the doctor found out. We are not victims of the weather. A lot of people are deceived.

·   ·   ·

Frederick L. Rawson, a great scientist in scientific prayer, spoke about a student of his who had a clairvoyant vision. She saw a plane on fire in her dream, and she and another woman went to pray in the area where she saw it. Lo and behold, they saw the plane come down, but they contemplated a presence of love and peace and harmony and beauty and right action in their minds and hearts, they were immersed in the whole omnipresence.

The plane came down, but these men were not burned. It was on fire, they were in a blazing furnace.

But in the higher levels of your mind, you can't be burned. They proved it. Surely, fire burns, yes, but not at higher levels.

When you tune into the infinite and reach the highest state of consciousness, you're immune. Neither does cancer have to kill you. If the person decides that he can ascend in consciousness, definitely believe, he will be healed. The psychic who appeared in this story died just a few years ago.

Not many people know about Virginia Graham's success in her famous TV show, *Girl Talk*, a show that came after she beat terminal cancer and made medical history. Her doctor explained the miracle Virginia experienced in these words: "She purified her bloodstream with her thoughts." Actually, this came about as a result of Virginia's fervent prayers when she knew she would be healed and would live.

"I have a surviving point of view," she claimed. "I am not interested in sinking or floating." This love of life communicates itself and is probably one of the reasons her TV show climbed to the top.

These great truths are there, of course. In the clairvoyant vision she saw this airplane come out of the clouds in flames. It burned out about one hundred feet from the ground, then cracked and fell. She looked about to see what the men were like. She couldn't distinguish anything about them. They were burned to a cinder in the dream.

Then the two women stood there praying. The airplane came out aflame, burned and cracked, just as she had seen. There were two men in it. But they were absolutely untouched. It was like the story of Shadrach, Meshach, and Abednego in the Bible. One of the men said, "I was about to throw myself out of the plane when suddenly a sense of absolute peace and safety came, and I sat back in the machine." There he was in a furnace.

That man turned out to be the son of the lady she had asked to come help her.

.   .   .

Down through the ages Indian fakirs have walked through fire under controlled conditions. Clifton Pierce, the research scholar, pointed out in his writings that in Surrey England in 1936, the English Society for Psychical Research ran a series of tests on two Indian fakirs imported expressly for the purpose.

The tests were graded by doctors, chemists, physicists, and psychologists at Oxford. The Indians walked the fire under controlled conditions, under the skeptical eyes of science. No chemicals were used. No preparations made. They repeated the performance under a variety of conditions over a period of several weeks.

Surface temperatures were between 450 and 500 degrees centigrade. The interior temperature, 1,400 degrees centigrade. There was no trickery or hallucination.

These examples are very common of course, and what Quimby wanted to bring out years ago was that sickness was of the mind. He said people contracted their infection in the church. They were given a guilt complex and fear that made them sick. He had to teach them a God of love because they had a belief in a punitive God, that God was punishing them.

For example, suppose a part of your body was severed, a limb or an arm put on a shelf. It couldn't catch cancer, tuberculosis, arthritis, ringworm, or any disease. Why? It is separated from the mind. It undergoes *dissolution*. Dissolution is not a disease. It's a matter of phenomenon.

Here were these doctors, out in the evening, in freezing temperatures, and yet they didn't catch a cold. They were supposed to get pneumonia, but because their minds were elsewhere in the higher state of mind. They had wounds, they had open lesions, but they failed to suppurate even though they were dirty.

The Indian fakir sleeps on a bed of nails because he's been hypnotized and told that whenever he pronounces a certain word, he can throw himself on a bed of nails and it will not penetrate the skin. I've seen that, you have too, probably. That's a conditioning process.

In 600 B.C. Lao-tzu said that when the sage goes forth into the jungle, he carries no sword or spear. He is not afraid of a javelin or the horn of a rhinoceros because there is no place in him where these can enter. In other words, he's built up an immunity. He's become intoxicated or seized by the divine antibody. So the externals are not causative, but man can make them a cause. And that's the great lie, that external things are causative. They're not.

*　　*　　*

Our eyes deceive us frequently. We see the sun, the moon, and the stars as well as each other by means of our eyes, which function in a manner similar to a camera. But don't judge according to appearances. Your five senses bring you an avalanche of sights and sounds and sundry concepts, most of which are negative.

Are you governed by your five senses during the day? Predictions of doom and gloom? Do you know when they mentioned the two vice presidents' wives had cancer, doctors told me that hundreds of women flocked to their offices out of fear?

That's why Quimby said, "You know, fear is behind this disease." They create the disease. "You tell a man who's never heard of the word cancer that he has cancer, it has no effect whatever upon him."

But, as Quimby pointed out, "You tell a man who's heard all the ravages of cancer, 'Look at this little lump. . . .' Maybe it's a harmless lump, maybe he fell down, maybe he hurt himself, but you tell him it's cancer, malignant, evil, he'll go home and he'll make it so."

Fear in his mind makes it so. *"That which I greatly feared has come upon me."* So don't judge according to appearances.

Physiologists tell us that when, for example, we look at a tree, its inverted images are reflected on the retina of our eyes, which transmit the picture to the brain centers in turn. These reactions are called visual impressions. The physiologist says that we see with the brain, you know that you see with your mind. You see with your eyes closed. You can see your mother if you close your eyes now. You can see colors better when your eyes are closed.

Vision is spiritual, eternal, indestructible. You see in your dreams. The faculty of clairvoyance is in all of us, though more highly developed in some. You're frequently deceived by what you look at. For example, a stick inserted in water appears broken. It isn't. When you stand on a railroad track, the two parallel lines of the rails seem to come together in the distance. White figures seem to be larger than black ones. Your eye deceives you.

Your eye often misrepresents the true state of existence because it deals only with the surface appearance. People say the sun rises and the sun sets. Actually, it neither rises nor sets. We see nothing as it is in reality because our eyes are geared to see according to our beliefs. If our eyes were geared in any other way, we would see things differently.

An airplane seems to move in a straight line. In reality, it follows a geometric arc. The razor blade with which you shave seems very sharp and straight, yet when seen under a microscope, it is a wavy line. It's not solid at all.

A piece of steel seems solid, yet scientists point out that X-rays reveal it to be porous, just like a body—that in reality it is made up of trillions of animated miniature universes, each having an extraordinarily rapid movement, yet no physical contact with each other.

If you looked at a photograph of your mother with a magnifying glass, her face would look like a succession of gray, black, and white points, depending on whether the paper is black, gray, or white. The portrait of your mother disappears. It only existed because your eyes were geared to a three-dimensional level.

You saw it on the scale of your accustomed observation. Looking at the razor blade with the eyes of science, we see electrons in perpetual motion that travel at the rate of several thousand miles per second.

Let's say you believe the stars are jinxed, that they're malignant or malefic, based on their configuration in the sky. Yet God pronounced everything he made and said it's good. It isn't the stars—it's your belief, as Quimby brought out. It's not the external thing. You're making an external thing a cause, but nothing's good or bad, only thinking makes it so. You made that law for yourself.

Let's say your sister was born a second before you were and you're identical twins. She has taken up the study of the science of mind, and she's leading a marvelous and wonderful life while you're suffering from your belief in malefic configurations of the planets and things are going upside down for you. Everything is going wrong because of that belief. Because whether you're consciously thinking of it or not, whatever you believe in your subconscious, it brings it about.

So it's a very dangerous thing to think that the planets are working against you. You made that belief, you're making an external thing a cause.

"The whole world believes a lie," Quimby said. "When I tell them the truth, they think I'm telling them a lie. They think God up there is punishing them."

The life principle can't punish you. It forgives you. You burn yourself, it forgives you, gives you new skin and tissue. If you cut yourself, it forms thrombin, gives you new skin. It always seeks to heal. The infinite cannot punish you.

Its eyes are too pure to behold iniquity. God is the eternal now. Now is the day of salvation. You're not a victim of karma. Nor are you a victim of the past. Because you're dealing with a timeless, faceless being, there's no past to worry about. The past is dead. Nothing matters but this moment.

Change this moment, and you change your destiny. Your beginning is a new end. The new beginning is when you enthrone Godlike ideas in your mind and live with them. The future is your present thinking grown up, and then the desert of your life will rejoice and blossom as the rose. That's the good news, the gospel, the truth, the being.

You change your mind now, and the martyr can be changed in the twinkling of an eye. We punish ourselves for our misuse of law.

Your five senses bring reports to you from the outside world which are not always true, but are oft times harmful and destructive. Parts that you emotionalize, accept as true, enter into your subconscious, and produce effects on your body and affairs according to thy nature.

. . .

There was a young man who believed a lie. He was gradually going blind. His doctor told him to leave the tailoring business, which was his vocation, because it caused a strain on his eyes, and to take a less arduous job. The ophthalmologist couldn't find anything radically wrong with the *fundus*, the part opposite the pupils of his eyes, and thought the difficulty might be emotional.

This young man was blaming his work and the result and strain on his eyes caused by sewing all day. He went to a psychic, and she made a chart for him. She said, "The planets are against you, Mars is square your sun," and so forth, and it frightened the life out of him. He thought the stars were against him now, though trouble was, it's not the stars. It's that we ourselves believe that we are underlings.

The real cause of his eye trouble was that he wanted to exclude his wife from his world. He said she was a nag, he hated to go home. But the trouble was within himself. Among his frequent expressions to me were, "I hate the sight of her. I can't stand to look at her. But I can't see my way out because I have two children and they need her. She won't give me a divorce, and I want the children."

His subconscious mind accepted his requests, these feelings and statements, and proceeded to respond by occluding his vision so that eventually he wouldn't be able to see. It had nothing to do with the planets, nothing to do with the tailoring business, nothing to do with the atmosphere.

You don't give power to external things. You give power to the Almighty that's within you, omnipotent supreme. There's nothing to oppose it, challenge it, thwart it, or vitiate it. You don't make a created thing a cause. That's why the whole world believes a lie.

I got this man and his wife together and explained the workings of the mind. She cooperated by ceasing to nag. They began to pray together, seeing God in each other. They also began to speak to one another kindly and lovingly. Moreover, they prayed every night and morning, alternating several selected Psalms—the 23rd, 27th, 46th, 91st, and 100th Psalms. The Psalms are songs of God, with meditations from *Quiet Moments With God*, a book of mine containing 60 special prayers.

In a month's time, his vision was back to normal. The ophthalmologist congratulated him. This man was certainly lying to himself by blaming his environment and his job, when all the time the true cause was in his destructive, negative emotions.

. . .

Disease means a lack of peace, a lack of ease. Disease is of the mind. Many people think disease is out there, that the body catches disease. That's why the world believes a lie. All disease is of the mind. Nothing happens in the body except what first happens in the mind.

The late Dr. Flanders Dunbar, a distinguished authority on psychosomatic medicine, was a medical doctor and a psychiatrist. And she also held degrees in religion. She discovered that a number of people were sick because of false religious beliefs.

I had a chat with a man who had been taking sedatives and observing a special diet for colitis, from which he had suffered for several years. He was lying to himself, as he blamed heredity and diet as the cause. "Colitis runs in my family. My grandmother and my mother had it also," he said. "I'm sure the food I eat has something to do with my trouble."

I pointed out to this man that Dr. Dunbar said that a number of cases of colitis in a New York Hospital showed that the men were tied to their mothers, and had never been away from their mothers for more than thirty days in their whole lives. None of these men were married, and the onset of their colitis was associated with the conflict between the mother tie and the desire for marriage.

The man had a similar conflict, plus a deep-seated resentment of his mother, who seemed to criticize and find fault with every girl he brought to their house as a prospective bride. It had nothing to do with heredity, it had nothing to do with diet. I found that he was deeply in love with a spiritual-minded young woman but hesitated to marry her lest he offend and disturb his mother.

His eventual solution was simple. He came to a decision to marry, bought a home for his bride, and broke the umbilical cord once and for all. He radiated love and goodwill to his mother and wished for all the blessings of Heaven, but he informed her that his wife now came first in his life.

His ulcerative colitis cleared up miraculously in a few weeks. He had been deceiving himself for several years, failing to see that the cause of his sickness was purely emotional, due to the poison pocket of resentment in the crevices of his soul. This man did not deliberately give himself colitis; his trouble came from the accumulation of his negative and destructive thinking.

What we need is spiritual food. You can eat the best food in the world and get up hungry from the table, hungry for love or peace or harmony. Don't you know that people eat the choicest food in the world? They have all the vitamins and the minerals, and still they die because of negative, destructive emotions. The negative emotion will turn that food you eat into poison. We need the bread of Heaven, the bread of peace and of harmony and of love. *Lord evermore, give us this bread.*

*   *   *

Because the subconscious mind is a law, it arranges all the deposited thoughts into a complex pattern. These subconscious patterns are not only the cause of all ills but also the cause of our successes and triumphant achievements.

The great lie is that the average man is constantly attributing causation outside himself. He blames conditions, environment, and circumstances. Sometimes he blames God, but all his difficulties are caused by mental patterns and beliefs lodged in his subconscious mind.

The great lie, in essence, is the belief in material causation. You will constantly hear people claim that material circumstances are the source of their difficulties, trials, and tribulations. But that isn't the thing they believe in. If you believe in a shrine, it isn't the shrine. It's your belief. It has nothing to do with the shrine.

If you think that if you bathe in a certain water you are going to be healed, it has nothing to do with the water. Analyze the water; it's the same water as in your own home. It's the belief, not the thing believed in.

Belief is living in the state of meaning, to be alive to something, to accept something as true. So the object of your faith, be it true or false, will give results. Some people say, "Well, if I touch the bone of that saint, I'll get a healing." So if somebody steals that bone, and they put a dog's bone there, and that person comes and thinks it's still the saint's bone, he'll get results. But not because of the bone. It's a dog's bone. Because of his belief. You can call it blind belief, the belief in the subconscious response. That's a simple law of life. Why people don't understand that today is beyond my imagination.

You'll constantly hear people say that circumstances, conditions, and all that are the source of their problems—as are other people. This is a lie of major importance. It must be utterly and completely refuted.

Talking with a woman some years ago, I learned her mother had a serious illness. She said her mother was a splendid Christian—most people don't know what that word means—that she was kindhearted, religious, and most generous. Why didn't God do something for her?

Such a question illustrates perfectly the great lie that affects many people. The law of life is the law of belief. We demonstrate what we believe. You can believe a lie, too, you know. Whatever we sow in our subconscious mind we shall reap. If we sow thoughts of sickness, fear, resentment, and enmity, we shall reap these things. To sow a thought Biblically speaking means to accept it wholeheartedly. It is our deep-seated beliefs that we demonstrate, what you really believe in your heart.

This woman and her mother were completely deceived in that both of them believed that sickness was independent of the mind. That it had nothing to do with the thinking process. That's the great lie that Quimby was talking about, that the whole world believes in, that sickness is out there somewhere, something they catch. That's too stupid for words.

Her mother had a bad heart condition and believed she could not be cured. That was a real belief, and so naturally she couldn't be healed. There are no incurable diseases; there are only incurable people. There are those who believe they cannot be healed, and according to their belief is it done unto them.

Her mother made excellent progress as she learned the law of life, as she ceased to be under the spell of the great lie that her heart is a material object with laws of its own, independent of her thinking. She now believes her body is subject to her thoughts and feelings. As she changes her mind, so she will change her body.

She's no longer that way. She knows how to pray, prays regularly and systematically, knowing that an infinite healing presence is flowing through her as the beauty of wholeness, vitality, and strength, that God's love dwells in her mind and body. She realized that sickness has no power beyond what she gives it in her own thoughts, and she found herself healed.

When trouble of any kind comes, look upon it as nature's signal that you're thinking wrongly in that direction. Then change your thought and keep it changed.

I've heard this expression, "What have I done to deserve this?" I was asked this by a young man, who added, "I have never done anything wrong." The explanation is the cure, as Quimby said in 1847.

I proceeded to point out to this young man that all our experiences are the result of our subconscious beliefs and assumptions. No matter what happens in your life, it is simply an outpouring of your subconscious mind. *"Out of the heart are the issues of life."*

The heart means your subconscious mind in Hebrew symbolism. All experiences, conditions, and events are the true experience, are the mathematical reproduction of subconscious patterns, of subconscious beliefs, and conditioning.

In other words, all the experiences, conditions, and events of our lives are the result of the totality of our beliefs. Moreover, all of us have many beliefs and ideas which we have long since forgotten, perhaps going back to childhood, hidden in the deeper recesses of our subconscious mind.

All our beliefs and tendencies with which we were born are still with us, and they have power to manifest in and influence our lives. For example, if you believe that sitting near a fan will give you a stiff neck, your subconscious mind will see to it that you get a stiff neck. Not because of the fan, which represents innocuous molecules of energy oscillating at a higher frequency, but because of your erroneous beliefs.

I've seen people in India operate working under a fan all day, and it has no effect whatever upon them. The fan is harmless. Surely you don't say the fan gives you a stiff neck. It's molecules moving in space.

If you're afraid that you'll catch a cold because someone sneezes, your fear is a movement of your own mind, which creates what you expect, fear, and believe. Others in the office don't get a cold. When the virus comes around, there are many men and women in your office and your factory who never get it. They don't believe in it. They believe in health.

If you happen to be in a warm room and you go out into the cool atmosphere, nature may cause you to sneeze. That's nature's way of bringing about a balance and equilibrium in your body. The sneeze is a blessing. It's a benediction. Many however fear that they're now catching a cold, not knowing it is the creative power of their own thought that caused the cold.

This young man wondered what he'd done to deserve such trouble. He confessed to me that he had bought an astrology magazine that morning, and it said there was great danger of an automobile accident, and to be very careful. He said that he was charged with fear and shook all over when he read it. He didn't want to drive that day, but he had to go for an audition, which was very important, and the only way was by car.

He had three crashes that same day, injuring one man seriously. He was suffering from shock himself and also received some contusions and lacerations. His car was badly damaged.

Job said, "What I greatly feared has come upon me." It had nothing to do with the stars or Mercury and Venus and harmony and Saturn. They're all molecules moving in space, like the earth. There's nothing evil in this universe. God pronounced everything good and very good.

Why should we have the effrontery, the audacity, the impertinence to pronounce certain things evil when God pronounced them good and very good? Nothing good nor bad, but thinking makes it so.

His great fear brought on these incidents, thoughts that were emotionalized and dramatized into experience by the subconscious mind. His subconscious mind took his great fear as a request and manifested it on the screen of space. What we sow, we shall surely reap. There's only one power. That's the spirit within you. You call it consciousness, which is the way you think, feel, and believe, which you give mental consent to. There's no other power, cause, or substance in the universe.

I gave this man a prayer to use regularly and elaborated on the point that if he filled his mind with these great truths, his subconscious mind would accept them accordingly. He would be under a subconscious compulsion to drive harmoniously and peacefully and nothing would ever happen to him again.

I suggested that he use the prayer regularly and systematically until it became a part of him, just like an apple becomes your bloodstream, the same way you learn to walk, to swim, to dance or play the piano, or to type. You repeat a thought pattern, act again and again. After a while, it is second nature, an automatic response of your deeper mind to your conscious mind, thinking, and acting. That's prayer.

When you type, you're praying. When you drive a car, you're praying. You're conforming to principles. The wheels have to be round. The gas won't drive your car. It has to change its consistency and become a vapor.

Likewise, in order for your world to change, you have to change your mind. You can't go on thinking the same old way. In order to begin to think in a new way, you have to get some new ideas. You have to find out about the laws of mind. You have to get a reason for your new thinking, and therefore you begin to think in whatsoever things that are lovely, noble, and God-like.

You realize your thoughts are creative. Whatever you impress into the subconscious, good or bad, is expressed, and therefore you begin to have a healthy, reverent, wholesome respect for your thoughts. There's a reason for your thinking then.

So this man began to affirm: This is God's car, his own car. It's God's idea. Of course it is. Where did it come from? It moves from point to point freely, joyously, and lovingly. God's wisdom guides this car in all its ways. God's order, symmetry, beauty govern the mechanism of this car at all times. God's holy presence blesses this car and all its occupants. The driver of this car is an ambassador of God. He's full of love and goodwill to all.

God's peace, truth, and understanding always governs the driver. God directs all decisions making the way straight, beautiful, and perfect. The spirit of the Lord God is upon the driver making all roads a highway for his God. A wonderful prayer.

There are many people who blame the weather for their colds, aches, and pains, also for their depression, their melancholia. Also they say, "You know, if only for that fellow in the office, I'd be promoted. He is blocking my good." You're making a god of another person. That's a big lie. There's only one God.

"Thou shall have no other gods before me. I, the Lord, thy God, am a jealous God." Jealous in the sense that you must not know another, because then your mind is double-minded. You're unstable. You're pressing up and down on the elevator. We don't know what you believe in. There's only one power, so you don't put another person on a pedestal and say, "You're a new God I have to worship. You're blocking my good."

Now, how on earth can you make any sense out of that? There's only one being, the infinite presence and power within you, nothing to oppose that. It's omnipotence, who created the world. "None can stay his hand, or say unto him, what doest thou?"

No one can oppose it. All powerful, the ever-living one, therefore if you want a promotion, you say to yourself, "Infinite spirit opens up a new door for me when I express myself at my highest level. When I exercise my faculties at the highest degree, and I have them all within wonderful income assisted with integrity and honesty, the promotion is mine."

Then you realize the power of the Almighty is backing you up. You go to the source. Stop believing in that big lie. The whole world believes a lie.

The air is harmless. Stop polluting the atmosphere with strange notions, false doctrines, and weird beliefs. When people talk about pollution, you never hear them talk about the pollution of the mind with resentment, hostility, and anger, and hate. You must learn the great truth that no person, situation, or condition causes you to be ill, unhappy, lonesome, or to suffer from pecuniary embarrassment.

There is no use in blaming somebody else. There's no one to blame at all. The beliefs and impressions made in your subconscious mind cause all your experiences and events of your life.

Someone can call you a skunk. Are you going to get angry and upset? Can't you say, "God's sister, you have no power to disturb me today. God's peace fills your soul." Or you can say to yourself, "God loves me and cares for me," and go on about your business. Can't you?

Don't tell me that person has power to disturb you. If so, you're suffering from the great lie, the biggest lie of all time. The suggestions and statements of others have no power to disturb you. You know that very well, except you're a mental case. You can curse or bless. It's the movement of your own mind, and there's no law preventing you from saying God loves me and cares for me.

You neutralize that negative thought or that angry thought. You make constructive energy out of it. You learn the great truth: No person, situation, or condition has any power to disturb you. Millions are suffering from the great lie because they're self-hypnotized by an accumulation of false ideas, beliefs, opinions, and sin's evidence.

Your subconscious mind acts as law to manifest and portray the accumulative patterns that are dwelling in your deeper mind. Nothing happens by chance. "Everything is pushed from behind," as Emerson said.

Psychiatrists and psychologists, and medical doctors delving and probing into your deeper mind, have demonstrated that you're not aware of these inner patterns. Not having knowingly placed them there, many persons assume they do not have them. Then, they establish alibis and excuses of all kinds to justify themselves.

Quimby proved 100 years ago that the body moves as moved upon. The body acts as acted upon. It has no volition, no self-conscious intelligence, no activity of itself. The body doesn't catch disease. That's insanity. The body is characterized by inertia. You can play a body of waves of light, molecules moving at tremendous speed. You can play in your body a melody of God or a hymn of faith. The body doesn't care.

It is characterized by inertia. It's an emotional disc upon which you play your emotions. If you sever a part of your body, as I explained to you previously, it can't suffer from a disease. It undergoes decomposition. I'd like to reiterate that because it's so true. Therefore all disease takes place in the mind, and disease is a lack of ease, lack of poise, lack of peace. That's why you read in the Bible He said, "Go in peace. Thy faith hath made thee whole." Why "in peace"? Because their mind was in turmoil, in sixes and sevens.

They were emotionally disturbed, overwrought, maybe jealous, envious, hateful, whatever it might be, but they had no peace of mind. If they had peace of mind, they couldn't be sick. Don't you know this? It's impossible to have a healthy mind and a sick body. "Mens sana, in corpore sano." A healthy mind, a healthy body. Very simple isn't it?

* * *

The great lie operates from many angles. There are those who blame the devil for their problems, but there's no such being. You know what the Hebrews

give that title for? It means "the eye," for the eye slays
a fact. Your eye deceives you. The earth moves around
the sun, or the earth is flat, your eye deceives you, so
they call the devil "the eye." They also call it laughter,
mirth, because there's no such being.

They say the devil has gone upside down. The
morbid, twisted, distorted concept that people have
of God of love, the pure impure. There's only one
power. There can't be two or three or a thousand, just
one. That's the way of all truth.

Devil, E-V-I-L. Spell it backwards, L-I-V-E. If
you're living life backwards, that's your evil, or your
devil. In Hebrew, "*sata*," Satan in the Book of Job,
means to slip, to err, to deviate from the truth. Surely,
that's your devil, when you deviate from the truth,
when you misuse the law. It's a misunderstanding, a
misinterpretation of life, wherever the universal presence and power diversifies itself. It limits itself, so we
see through a glass darkly. Your misunderstanding is
the only devil there is. Or you can call it ignorance,
another word for it. Buddha called it ignorance. It
means living life backwards. Spell "live" backwards
and that's what you have.

The ancient Hebrew mystics said the devil is one
who lies about God, a slanderer. Those slanderers tell
lies about the truths or the infinite. Good and evil are

simply the movements of your mind relative to the living spirit within you, which is God.

The forces of nature are not evil. It depends entirely on the use we make of the elements of nature and the forces within us, whether we have a constructive or a negative reaction. The great lie is to enthrone the idea in our mind that things, conditions, and phenomena are the determining causes of your misery, suffering, and misfortune. It's the biggest lie of all time.

There is no one to change but yourself, and you are your own savior. To think that some man is going to save you is the biggest lie in the world because your Bible tells you, point blank, "I rejoice in God, my savior." There's only one God. There can't be two Gods or two powers, it's impossible spiritually, mentally, and any other way.

I say your gods and all your sons are the most high. Everybody is a son of God. We're all expressions of the one being, the one progenitor. So, stop giving power to people, conditions, and events.

A banker said to me one time that members of his staff were out due to a viral infection, that he was afraid of catching it as well. He wanted to know how to protect himself. I told him that he was afraid of an invisible virus that he couldn't see, that had no power over him. I pointed out that he was suggesting to himself that he might be liable to the infection, that the suggestions and statements of others had no power to create the things they suggested.

The power is in you, the movement of your own thought: *"Choose ye this day whom ye will serve. Hold before you this day a blessing and a curse; a blessing if you obey the law, a curse if you disobey."*

The suggestions of others are powerless. I told him to reject the suggestion of infection completely, that the creative action is always of his own thought and feeling. I also pointed out that nothing can happen to him except through the creative power of his own mind, that others therefore had no power. He affirmed frequently as follows:

> I and my Father are one. I live now and have my being in God. God lives, moves, and has His being in me. God can't be sick. The spirit was never hurt nor wounded. What is true of God is true of me. God can't be sick. Therefore, I can't be sick. I am all health. God is my health. Health is mine. Joy is mine. Peace is mine. I feel wonderful.

You can rest assured, he had no flu. You're in charge of your own mind, and you have the wonder-ful opportunity to affirm that God's peace and love fills your heart, your mind, and your whole being. The power is always in you, not in the other.

"*Thou shalt have no other gods before me. I am the Lord. That is my name. My glory you shall not give to another. Neither shall you give my praise. I am the Lord, and there is none else.*"

From the rising of the sun to the setting of the same, there is none else. When you say *I am*, you're announcing the presence and power of God within yourself. Pure being, life awareness. It's the only presence, power, cause, and substance.

The big lie is to give power to any person, place, or thing; germ, circumstance, or condition. Then you're no longer loving the one, the beautiful, and the good. "*Thou shalt have no other gods before me.*"

Cease giving power and prerogatives to people, conditions, and events that have no power. Cease looking upon matter as evil or the world as evil. Spirit and matter are one. Matter is the lowest degree of spirit, and spirit is the highest degree of matter. Matter and invisible energy are one. Scientists inform us that energy and matter are interchangeable. Energy and matter are one.

This is why thoughts are things. Thought is cause. The manifestation is the effect. There is a wonderful prayer, and prayer changes things. It changes the person who prays.

"The Lord is my light and my salvation. Whom shall I fear? The Lord is the strength of my life. Of whom shall I be afraid?" This one verse of the 27th Psalm gives you personal freedom from all fear. It reveals to you the source of all power, strength, and wisdom. It enables you to reject the power of externals. It takes the burden off your shoulders, sets you on the high road to peace of mind, health, and happiness.

The Lord is the presence of God, the "I am" within you, given to you in the 3rd Book of Exodus. The Lord is your own consciousness, your own awareness, your own life principle, your state of consciousness, the way you think, feel, believe, and the meaning behind your belief. God in the midst of you is guiding you now. His peace fills your soul. God's love saturates your whole being. I am the Lord that healeth thee.

"I am the Lord, thy God. I will come and heal thee." God be with you.

The Secret of
I Am That I Am

n the third chapter of Exodus, we read these words:

"*I am the Lord, thy God, which have brought thee out of the land of Egypt, out of the house of bondage. Thou shalt have no other gods before me.*"

"*God said to Moses, 'Come now, therefore, and I will send thee to Pharaoh that thou mayest bring forth my people, the children of Israel, out of Egypt.'*

"*Moses said unto God, 'Who am I that I should go unto Pharaoh, and that I should bring forth the children of Israel out of Egypt?' Moses said unto God, 'Behold when I come unto the children of Israel, and shall say unto them, "The God of your fathers hath sent me," and they shall say to me, "What is his name?" What shall I say unto them?'*

"*God said unto Moses, 'I Am that I Am,' and he said, 'Thus shalt thou say unto the children of Israel, "I Am hath sent me unto you." Thus shalt thou say unto the children of Israel, "the Lord of God of your fathers, the God of Isaac, the God of Abraham, and the God of Jacob hath sent me unto you. This is my name forever, and this is my memorial for all generations."'*

When you say *I Am*, you are announcing the presence of the living God within you. You are declaring yourself to me. I Am that I Am. The word "that" indicates *that* which you want to be, *that* which you would like to be. The second "I Am" means the answered prayer, achievement and fulfillment of your desire, dream, or aspiration. You do not repeat *I Am that I Am* parrot-like. You feel yourself to be what you long to be.

You become interested, fascinated, absorbed in your ideal. It begins to gel in your mind, and whatever is impressed in the subconscious is impressed upon the screen of space. Then comes the cry of victory, the wholeness, beauty, and perfection of the thing you want it to be.

You can say for example, "I am illumined. I am inspired. I am divinely guided. I am made whole." You can live in that atmosphere because whatever you attach to I Am, you become. Whatever you attach to I Am with feeling and understanding, you will become that very thing.

If you're looking for your true place in life, this is a simple prayer, but it works in a magnificent, wonderful way. I have given it to many people throughout the world. Say to yourself, "I am in my true place. I am doing what I love to do. I am divinely happy. I am divinely prospered."

Say that feelingly, knowingly, and meaningfully, and the deeper mind will take over and open up all doors for you. Your hidden talents will be revealed to you, the door will open up, and you will find yourself in your true place, meaning you will be expressing yourself at your highest possible level.

I Am means awareness, being, life principle, unconditioned consciousness. The Hindus use the word *aum*, it's the same thing. It means the limitless one. It means the holy one who inhabited the eternity, whose name is perfect.

You can say, for example, "I am whole. I am perfect. I am vital. I am strong." The Bible says, *"Let the weak say I am strong. Let the widow say it as well."* Take your attention away from your problem, whether it's sickness, lack, limitation—be it what it may. Focus your attention on your ideal, your goal, your objective.

Claim yourself to be what you long to be. Rejoice and feel it, and then the old condition will pass away, and you will experience the joy of the answered prayer. The Bible says, "Behold, I"—meaning the infinite—"make all things new."

The Bible says, *"Ye shall not need to fight in this battle. Set yourself, stand still, and see the salvation of the Lord."* The word *salvation* is an old Hindu term meaning a solution to your problem, the answer to your prayer. It means "saved."

Saved from what? From fear, ignorance, superstition. You're saved from sickness, disease, lack, limitation of all kinds. Why? Because you're aware of the God presence within and your capacity to contact it. When you call upon it, it answers you. It will be with you in trouble. It will set you on high because you hath known its name. Its name is nature, the way it works.

"Behold, I stand and knock at the door. If any many will hear my voice and open the door, I will come in and sup with him, and he with me." The God presence is always knocking at the door of your heart. It's always seeking to express itself at higher levels through you. You're a channel of the divine, and therefore, you must listen to the murmurings and whisperings of your heartstrings, because God is forever saying to you, "Come on up higher. I have need of you at higher levels."

Therefore your desire is a gift of God. The realization of your desire is your savior. If you were lost in the woods, divine guidance or the light of God would illumine your pathway and reveal to you the way out. If you're hungry, food is your savior. If you're dying of thirst in the desert, water is your savior. If you're in prison, freedom is your savior. If you're sick, health is your savior.

The answer is always within you, and the saving consciousness is within you, because God grows in you. *"I rejoice in God, my savior,"* the Bible says.

"Stand still and see the salvation of the Lord," which means to quiet the wheels of your mind. Call upon this infinite intelligence which responds to you. If you ask for a fish, it will not give you a serpent. If you ask for bread, it will not give you a stone. It becomes the embodiment of your ideal.

Have a deep conviction that all is well in spite of all the reasons why the condition seems to be impossible. Remain unmoved. Live in the atmosphere of victory, and victory will be yours. Having seen the end, you have willed a means to the realization of that end. Contemplate the happy ending. Realize and know that all the power of God will flow to the focal point of attention.

I am a pure, unconditioned being. It is the creative power. It deals with the infinity of God. Another way of explaining it is this: "I" means the infinite. "A" comes from "Ab," meaning the father, and "M" means the mother. In other words, the infinite is the father and mother of God, the male and female principle.

The ancient Hebrews said that God, in order to create, divided himself into two, male and female. Then God conceived Himself to be the sun, the moon, and the stars. He believed Himself to be man, pictured Himself as man, and all these archetypes were given to the female aspect of Himself. This is called the womb of God, which created all things in sequence and brought forth all things in this universe.

All things were made that way, and there was nothing made that was not made that way. You're created the same way, you're male and female too. Your conscious mind is the male, and your subconscious is the female. Whatever you impregnate or impress upon the subconscious, the female aspect of yourself, the subconscious brings forth, good, bad, or indifferent.

You may say I'm a man, I'm an Englishman, I'm a Scotsman, I'm an attorney, I'm a doctor, I'm a Republican, I'm a Democrat. These are facts about yourself, but they are limitations of the infinite one, for God is limitless. In other words, you're the conditioned state of the unconditioned being.

These states I just mentioned are constructive expressions of the infinite, but God is unlimited. It is pure, unconditioned being. It is the limitless one, the Holy One of Israel, it's called.

To say that God is anything in particular implies limitation or circumscription. God is infinite, man is something particular. Man is the individualization of God consciousness.

Emerson said, "Every man is God walking the earth." In other words, God became man by believing Himself to be man. Man is God, in limitation.

Therefore you were born with certain talents and abilities. You're unique, there's no one in all the world like you, because you are you. Perhaps you're mechanically inclined. Perhaps you're musically inclined. Perhaps you're spiritually inclined, and so on. There are no two blades of grass alike, no two crystals of snow and no two veins on a tree alike, or two leaves.

Infinite differentiation is the law of life. Some men are tall, some are short. Some are very fat, some are thin. Some are born blind, some are crippled, and so on. We're all equal in the eyes of God, but men are not equal in strength or wisdom or understanding or anything else.

You can also attach negative things to I Am. Remember that whatever you attach to I Am with feeling, you'll become. You can say, "I am dumb. I am inferior. I am rejected. I am no good. I am sick. I am frustrated. I am lonesome. I am unhappy. I am poor." All these things will come to pass as you continue to reiterate them, because they sink down from your conscious to your subconscious mind, and just like seeds, they grow after their time. So be sure that you do not attach anything to I Am that is not noble, Godlike, and dignified.

·   ·   ·

"*Seek ye first the Kingdom of God and his righteousness, and all things shall be added unto you.*" What does that mean? The Kingdom of Heaven, or the Kingdom of God, is within yourself. It's your own consciousness. It's your awareness of being. It's the invisible part of you. It's your mind, your consciousness, your thoughts, your imagination, your feeling, your beliefs.

Your state of consciousness is what you think and believe. It's what you feel. It's what you imagine yourself to be. Therefore your state of consciousness is whatever you think, feel, believe, and give mental consent to. All these things are dramatized on the screen of space.

Your consciousness is the only God, the only creative power, because it's the invisible part of you. It's your thought and feeling, which creates your destiny. These are elements of divinity, and your consciousness is the sum total of your conscious and subconscious thinking, feeling, and believing.

You first go within your own consciousness, your own mind. There you claim to be what you want to be, and that spirit within you will honor, validate, and execute it. Go within, shut the door of your senses, and pray to your Father, which is in secret. The Father is the creative power, it's the progenitor. It's the life principle within you. It's the source of all things.

*　*　*

"In the beginning was the Word, and the Word was with God, and the Word was God." The Word is the thought expressed. You're told the Word was God too, because it's created.

If you hypnotize a man, put your finger on his neck and say, "This is a red-hot poker," he'll get a blister, won't he? He'll have changes in the autonomic nervous system. You'll actually see a blister. In other words, the beginning and the end are the same. The thought and the manifestation are one. Thoughts are things, and what you feel, you attract, and what you imagine, you become.

Whatever you want, you go to consciousness for it. That's the meaning of *"Seek ye first the Kingdom of Heaven."* The righteousness, the right use of the law.

Your concept of yourself determines your future. Your world is called good and very good because it is the likeness of the consciousness which made it. For example, the law of the Lord is perfect, because if you're conscious of being one thing, and then you express something other than what you claim and feel and believe to be true, that would be a violation of the law. It wouldn't be good.

Isn't it natural for an apple seed to become an apple tree? Seeds grow after their kind. Therefore, if you feel one thing in your heart, and you express something else on the screen of space, that would be a violation of the law of being. If a man is full of hatred, resentment, hostility, and ill will, he certainly can't express love, peace, beauty, or joy.

These negative emotions get snarled up in the subconscious, and being negative must have a negative outlet. The law is not being broken; the law, we said, is always perfect. It brings forth the likeness of man's conception of himself. All the divisions in the world are projections of the one, the beautiful, and the good.

The absolute can't contain within itself, something which is not itself. Otherwise it would not be the absolute. The absolute comes from *Ab*, the father, meaning that the whole world and everything you see comes out of the absolute, comes out of the one. There's only the one.

The ancient Hebrews defined it this way:

"Ever the same in my inmost being, eternal, absolutely one, whole, complete, perfect, indivisible, timeless, shapeless, and ageless, without face, form, or figure. The silent, brooding presence, fixed in the hearts of all men. I am the virgin snow on the mountaintop. I am the fruit and the valley depths. I am the gold and the salve on the altars dedicated to the gods. Yea, I am the mire left on the

sandals by the fateful at the temple gate. Hear me
and see me in all, oh man of God, and thou shall
see indeed."

That is to say, every single thing you see is God
made manifest, God appearing as the sun, the moon,
the stars, the trees, the mud, the earth. This is God
becoming all these things, *"For God thinks, and worlds
appear."*

You can say, "I am" to announce the presence
of God. Whenever you say "I am," remember you're
announcing the presence of the living God within
you. *"The word is nigh in the mouth and thy heart, to will
and to do."*

People down through the ages have looked for
the Holy Grail. They've looked for the lost word, the
philosopher's stone, and all the time, the word is in
their mouth a thousand times a day. It's called, "I am,"
announcing pure being, the reality of you, the living
spirit within you.

It was never born; it will never die. Water wets it
not, fire burns it not, wind blows it not away. It is the
reality of you. That's a wonderful thing to know, a
marvelous thing to realize.

*   *   *

The Bible says, *"Happy is the man that condemneth not himself and that which he alloweth."* In other words, stop condemning yourself. Realize that you can now claim what you want to be. You can claim that you possess what you long to possess. You can claim that you're doing what you long to do. You can live in that mental atmosphere that will gradually sink down by osmosis from your conscious to your subconscious. It will become a conviction as you nourish it and sustain it.

Then your limitation will disintegrate, and you will rise like the phoenix from the ashes of the old. You'll become a new man because, "I must die to what I am before I can live to what I long to be."

That's why Paul says, "I die daily." You must die to the belief in poverty and resurrect the belief in God's opulence. Die to the belief in sickness and believe it's God's will for you that you be happy, joyous, and free, vital and strong. Claim that the wholeness of God is flowing through you.

Take your attention away from the multitude of reasons why you can't achieve something and focus your attention on your ideal. Nourish and sustain it. The answer will come. Keep on keeping on, and the day will break, and all the shadows will flee away.

Remember that God is the living spirit within you, moving as unity. God is all bliss, all peace, all harmony, all joy, all love, boundless wisdom, infinite intelligence, and indescribable beauty. God is called many names, Allah, Brahma, Jehovah, El Shaddai Adonai. There are sixty-seven names in the Psalms given to God, but they deal with powers and attributes of God, for God has no name.

You cannot contact the God presence within if you're full of cruelty, self-pity, condemnation, or ill will. When you pray, you're told forgive if you ought against any, so that your Heavenly Father may forgive you. If you come to the altar to offer your gift, the Bible tells you that if you have fought against your brother, come and make friends with your brother. Come and offer your gift, but your gift is your desire, and the altar is your own mind where you walk and talk with God.

The only gift you can give God is praise and thanksgiving. Come into His presence singing, come into His courts with praise. Be thankful unto Him, and bless His name. But you must come unspotted. There must be no spot in thee. *"Thou art all fair, my love. There is no spot in thee,"* for love is the fulfilling of the law, the law of health, of happiness, and peace.

Therefore when you go to God, you must be full of love and goodwill, and love is an outreaching of the heart. It's an emanation of goodwill. It is wishing for all men what you wish for yourself. Wish for those who hurt you love, peace, harmony, joy, and all the blessings of life. You know when you've forgiven because there is no sting in your mind.

If you had an abscess a year ago, perhaps it was very painful. Maybe the doctor lanced it, and you have no pain now. You have a memory, but no sting. That's forgiveness.

If you heard of some marvelous news about someone who cheated you, said unkind things about you, or undermined you and it stung, it means the roots of hatred are still there in your subconscious mind, playing havoc with you. Because the healing power of God does not flow through a contaminated consciousness, no more so than water flows through a sink when the pipe is all stopped up. Perhaps the sink is full of corrosion, or rust or debris or sand or something. The plumber comes and removes it, but the water was always waiting to flow through.

Likewise, the healing power of God is within you. You don't create it. It's called the Holy Spirit, the spirit of wholeness, and all disease is fragmentation, separation from the divine. Therefore you must be in a state of purity and wholeness when you go to God. That's love.

Then you'll get an answer. Then the healing will come. The Bible said, *"In the beginning, God."* In other words, put God first in your life. Do you put something before God? Do you say, "I'm too busy?" Are you saying you're too busy for God?

· · ·

Do not give power to any created thing. Do not give power to sticks or stones or stars or suns or moons or men or conditions or circumstances. Everything is subject to change. The thinker is greater than the thought. The artist is greater than his art. The Creator is greater than his creation.

The scientific thinker does not give power to any created thing in this universe. He does not give power to the phenomenalistic world or anything contained. He gives allegiance, devotion, and loyalty to the I Am within him, the only presence, the only power, the only cause, the only substance.

The minute you give power to any other thing in the world, you're practicing idolatry. It's sometimes referred to in our Bible as adultery, but these words are synonymous. You're cohabitating with evil, in the bed of your own mind.

Remember the great truth, *"I am the Lord, thy God. Thou shalt have no other gods before me."* Put God first and everything will go right in your life. The reason for so much chaos and confusion in your life, if there is any chaos, confusion, sickness, or poverty, is because you're putting something else before God.

In the beginning, God. Before you go to work in the morning, sit down and ask for God's guidance, right action. Claim the peace, love, and harmony of God are flooding your mind, your heart, and your whole being. There is but one power, the only presence, the only cause, and the only substance. It's an old truth, called the burning bush in the Bible.

The Bible says, *"I Am hath sent me unto you."* It's the burning bush, because it's the everlasting light. It was never born; it will never die. It's the presence of God in you. It had no beginning and end. *"I am without beginning and without end, older than night or day, younger than the babe newborn, brighter than light, darker than darkness, beyond all things and creatures, yet fixed in the hearts of all men."*

It's a magnificent truth, isn't it? *"I Am hath sent me unto you."* When some engineers, physicists, or scientists have a difficult problem, a so-called insurmountable difficulty, they say, "I Am hath sent me. God sent me here to solve this problem and overcome it." They say, "The problem is here, but God is here, too, and the problem is divinely outmatched." Because the infinite intelligence and boundless wisdom of God knows only the answer.

You don't go to God with a problem. You go to God with the answer, for God knows only the answer, and as you realize that the light of God shines in you and that God reveals to you the answer, you grapple with it courageously. The ideas, the wisdom, the intelligence, the power, the strength, all these things are given to you. Go right ahead and grapple with the problem, courageously knowing in your heart and soul that all the power of God will respond to that attitude of mind.

· · ·

Remember any description of God, or any definition of God, is limitation. Spinoza said, "To define God is to deny Him," because you can't define the infinite being. So remember, your I Am is your true being. It's your real nature, it's the self of you. Remember also that no one can say "I Am" for you. *"You're first in the pool,"* as the Bible says. *"You're first in the holy omnipresence. No one can get in before you."* You read that in the Book of John.

No person, place, or thing, or condition, or circumstance can thwart your good. There is no power in all the world, no person in all the world can prevent the flow of your thoughts, your feelings, your imagery, or this flow of the spirit in you. It is Almighty. It's mighty overall that your real identity is the presence of God in you. Whatever you attach to I Am with conviction, that you are and that you have.

Don't ever say, "I can't." Don't ever say, "I'm too weak." Don't ever say, "There's no way out." Instead say, "I Am hath sent me here." If there's discord in the office, if there's difficulty in your home, if you have an emotional problem or sickness, say, "God is here, and God can show me the way. God can heal me." Then the road will open up. You'll surmount all the difficulties.

God doesn't sit upon a throne up in the heavens. A throne simply means your authority, the power itself. God is pure spirit, infinite creative life, infinite mind, infinite intelligence, boundless wisdom. When the Bible says, *"God spake unto Moses,"* it simply means that Moses was in meditation, calling upon the God presence for inspiration and guidance. When his inspiration came to him, the intuitive sense welled up within him. Intuition is taught from within. Therefore, the inspiration began to flow, and Moses began to write, *"In the beginning, God created the heavens and the earth, and the earth was without form or void, and darkness was upon the face of the deep."*

Remember that the Bible writers were inspired. They were past masters in the art of psychology in the story of the soul. They knew the great laws of minds and the way of the spirit. They spoke in parables, allegories, fables, myths, cryptograms, and numbers. They spoke in Kabbalistic language.

Don't ever say, "I'm afraid. I am weak. I'm no good." You're destroying yourself. Don't ever say, "I'm fearful, or I'm worried, or I'm jealous, or I'm critical." When you do, you're shortening your life, and your cells become more sensitive to pain.

Say, "I am one with God. One with God is a majority. God loves me and cares for me. The love of God surrounds me and enfolds me. I bear a charmed life. Divine loves goes before me, making straight and perfect my way." When you do that, you are lengthening your life, and you begin to lead a charmed life.

Emerson said, "All successful men have agreed in one thing, in being causationists." They believe that things were not by luck, but by law, and that there was not a weak or cracked link in the chain that joins the first and the last of things, the cause and the effect. Shallow men believe in luck. Wise and strong men believe in cause and effect.

Mark Twain said, "Fortune knocks at every man's door, but in a good many cases, the man is in a neighboring saloon, and does not hear her."

Man must be alert and alive. He must take advantage of the opportunities all around him. Man must not expect to be rewarded for indolence, apathy, or slothfulness.

The aphorism "As a man thinketh in his heart, so is he," sets forth and portrays all the experiences and conditions of man's life. Man is what he thinks all day long, and his character is the totality of this thinking. Cause and effect are as absolute and undeviating in the hidden realm of thought as in the world of visible and material things.

"*I Am alpha and omega. I am the first and the last.*" The cause and effect are the same. Action and reaction are the same. "*I am the Lord, God of all flesh. I am the Lord, thy God, and from the rising of the sun, to the setting of the same, there is none else.*" That's a magnificent truth, isn't it?

Realize that your consciousness, your own I Amness is the only presence, the only power, the only cause, the only substance. Everything is made inside and out of it. It is the only being in all the world.

Man's joy and suffering are the reflections of his habitual thinking. Thus does a man garner the sweet and bitter experiences in his life. In order to experience good fortune, realize that you are the master of your thoughts, emotions, and reactions in life. You are the maker and shaper of your conditions, experiences, and events. Every thought felt as true, allowed to be accepted as true by our conscious mind, takes root in your subconscious mind, blossoms sooner or later into an act, and bears its own fruit of opportunity and experience.

Good thoughts bring forth good fruit; bad thoughts harvest bad fruit. It is not a cruel fate that sends a man to jail or to the poorhouse, but it is the pathway of vicious, destructive, or criminal thinking which he had been secretly fostering in his heart. When these reached a point of saturation in his subconscious mind, they were precipitated into external experiences, fashioned after the image and likeness of his negative thinking.

Fall in love with a higher image of yourself, the God-self within you. Exalt God in the midst of you. When any fear comes into your mind, say, "I exalt God in the midst of me." There is no fear in love. There is no fear in God, for God is the only power.

All fear is based upon suppositional opposites to God. That is, you're placing another power. There isn't any other power. That's the cause of all fear in this world. Some people believe in the devil, evil powers, and so forth. There's only one power. It moves as unity and is harmony. It moves as love and as life.

ABOUT THE AUTHOR

Born in 1898 on the southern coast of Ireland, JOSEPH MURPHY grew up in a large, devout Catholic family. Murphy's parents urged him to join the priesthood but as a young seminarian he found religious doctrine and catechism too limiting. Eager to peer more deeply into the internal mechanics of life, Murphy left seminary to dedicate his energies to chemistry, which he studied both before and after his religious training.

In the early 1920s, married yet still searching for his place in the world of career and commerce, Murphy relocated to America to seek employment as a chemist and druggist. After running a pharmacy counter at New York's Algonquin Hotel, Murphy renewed his study of mystical and metaphysical ideas. He read the works of Taoism, Confucianism, Transcendentalism, Buddhism, Scripture—and New Thought. The seeker grew fully enamored of the New Metaphysics sweeping the Western world. The causative power of thought, Murphy came to believe, revealed the authentic meaning of the world's religions, the deeper meaning of psychology, and the eternal laws of life.

In arriving at his matured spiritual outlook, Murphy told an interviewer that he studied in the 1930s with the same teacher who tutored his contemporary New Yorker and friend, mystic Neville Goddard (1905–1972). Murphy said they shared the same teacher: a turbaned man of black-Jewish descent named Abdullah.

In the late-1930s, Murphy began his climb as a minister and writer, soon lecturing on the radio and speaking live on both coasts. He wrote prolifically on the autosuggestive and causative faculties of thought, and reached a worldwide audience in 1963 in *The Power of Your Subconscious Mind*, which went on to sell millions of copies and has remained one of the most enduring books on positive-mind philosophy.

After a career spanning dozens of books and thousands of lectures on positive-mind philosophy, Murphy died in 1981 in Laguna Hills, CA.

JOSEPH MURPHY TIMELINE

1898: Joseph Denis Murphy is born on May 20, the fourth of five children (three girls and two boys) to a devout Catholic family on the Southern Coast of Ireland in Ballydehob, County Cork. Murphy's father was headmaster of a local boys high school.

Circa 1914–1915: After being educated locally, Murphy studies chemistry in Dublin. Bowing to his parents' wishes he enrolls briefly in a Jesuit seminary. Dissatisfied with his studies, and unbelieving of the doctrine of no salvation outside the church, Murphy leaves seminary.

Circa 1916–1918: Murphy works as a pharmacist for England's Royal Army Medical Corps during World War I.

1918–1921: Murphy works as a pharmacist in Dublin. He earns a monthly salary of about $10.

1922: Dissatisfied with traditional religion and finding limited opportunities to practice as a chemist, Murphy just shy of age 24 arrives in New York City on April 17,

1922. He is accompanied by his wife, Madolyn, who is eight years his senior (wedding date unknown). He arrives with $23. Applies for citizenship in August.

1923–1938: Murphy works as a pharmacist in New York City including at a pharmacy counter at the Algonquin Hotel. He deepens his study into metaphysics and years later recounts having studied with the figure of Abdullah, a black man of Jewish descent whom Murphy's contemporary and fellow New Yorker, Neville Goddard (1905–1972), wrote that he studied with. Murphy reports that Abdullah tells Murphy that he actually had three brothers, not two. Upon checking with his mother, Murphy discovers that he had a third brother who died at birth and was never spoken of.

Circa 1931: Murphy begins attending the Church of the Healing Christ in New York City, presided over by Emmet Fox.

Circa 1938: Murphy is ordained as a Divine Science minster. He continues to work as a druggist and chemist.

1941: Murphy begins broadcasting metaphysical sermons over the radio.

1942: Murphy enlists as a pharmacist in the New York State National Guard, a post he holds until 1948.

1943: Murphy studies Tarot in New York City and comes to believe in symbolic correspondences between the Tarot cards and Scripture.

1945: Murphy writes his first book, *This Is It: The Art Of Metaphysical Demonstration.*

1946: Murphy is ordained as a Religious Science Minister in Los Angeles. He soon takes over the pulpit of the Institute for Religious Science in Rochester, New York. He publishes the short works *Wheels of Truth, The Perfect Answer,* and *Fear Not.*

1948: Murphy publishes *St. John Speaks, Love is Freedom,* and *The Twelve Powers Mystically Explained.*

1949: Murphy is re-ordained into Divine Science and becomes minister of the Los Angeles Divine Science Church, a post he will hold for the next 28 years. Services become so popular that they are held at the Wilshire Ebell Theater.

1952: Publishes *Riches Are Your Right.*

1953: Publishes *The Miracles of Your Mind, The Fragrance of God,* and *How to Use the Power of Prayer.*

1954: Publishes *The Magic of Faith* and *The Meaning of Reincarnation,* one of his most controversial books.

1955: Publishes *Believe in Yourself* and *How to Attract Money*, one of his most enduringly popular works.

1956: Murphy writes *Traveling With God* in which he recounts his international speaking tours, comparing New Thought with various global traditions. He also publishes *Peace Within Yourself* (*St. John Speaks* revised) and *Prayer Is the Answer*.

1957: Publishes *How to Use Your Healing Power*.

1958: Publishes the short works *Quiet Moments with God, Pray Your Way Through It, The Healing Power of Love, Stay Young Forever, Mental Poisons and Their Antidotes*, and *How to Pray With a Deck of Cards*.

1959: Publishes *Living Without Strain*.

1960: Publishes *Techniques in Prayer Therapy*.

1961: Publishes *You Can Change Your Whole Life* and *Nuclear Religion*.

1962: Publishes *Why Did This Happen to Me?*

1963: Publishes *The Power of Your Subconscious Mind*, which becomes a worldwide bestseller and a landmark of New Thought philosophy. The book's publication makes Murphy into one of the most widely known metaphysical writers in the world.

1964: Publishes *The Miracle of Mind Dynamics*.

1965: Publishes *The Amazing Laws of Cosmic Mind Power*.

1966: Publishes *Your Infinite Power to Be Rich*.

1968: Publishes *The Cosmic Power Within You*.

1969: Publishes *Infinite Power for Richer Living*.

1970: Publishes *Secrets of the I Ching*.

1971: Publishes *Psychic Perception: The Magic of Extrasensory Perception*.

1972: Publishes *Miracle Power for Infinite Riches*

1973: Publishes *Telepsychics: The Magic Power of Perfect Living*.

1974: Publishes *The Cosmic Energizer: Miracle Power of the Universe*.

1976: Murphy's first wife Madolyn dies. He marries his secretary, Jean L. Murphy (nee Wright), also a Divine Science minister. He writes *Great Bible Truths for Human Problems*.

1977: Publishes *Within You Is the Power*

1979: Publishes *Songs of God*

1980: Publishes *How to Use the Laws of Mind*

1981: Murphy dies on December 16 in Laguna Hills, CA, where he and his wife Jean are living at the Leisure World retirement community, now known as Laguna Woods Village.

1982: *These Truths Can Change Your Life* is published posthumously.

1987: Canadian writer Bernard Cantin publishes the French language work *Joseph Murphy se raconte à Bernard Cantin* [*Joseph Murphy Speaks to Bernard Cantin*] with Quebec's Éditions Un Monde Différent. The book is based on an extended series of interviews Cantin conducted with Murphy before his death and provides a rare window into Murphy's career. It does not appear in English. *The Collected Essays of Joseph Murphy* is published posthumously.